CliffsNotes™

Paradise Lost

By Bob Linn, Ph. D.

IN THIS BOOK

- Learn about the Life and Background of the Author
- Preview an Introduction to the Poem
- Study a graphical Character Map
- Explore themes and literary devices in the Critical Commentaries
- Examine in-depth Character Analyses
- Enhance your understanding of the work with Critical Essays
- Reinforce what you learn with CliffsNotes Review
- Find additional information to further your study in CliffsNotes Resource Center and online at www.cliffsnotes.com

Wiley Publishing, Inc.

About the Author

Bob Linn is Chairman of the English Department at Calhoun High School in Calhoun, Georgia. He has a Ph.D. from the University of South Carolina.

Publisher's Acknowledgments

Editorial

Project Editor: Tracy Barr

Acquisitions Editor: Greg Tubach

Glossary Editors: The editors and staff at Webster's New World™ Dictionaries

Editorial Administrator: Michelle Hacker

Composition

Indexer: York Production Services, Inc.

Proofreader: York Production Services, Inc.

Wiley Indianapolis Composition Department

CliffsNotes™ *Paradise Lost*

Published by:
Wiley Publishing, Inc.
111 River Street
Hoboken, NJ 07030
www.wiley.com

Table of Contents

How to Use This Book

This CliffsNotes study guide on Milton's *Paradise Lost* supplements the original literary work, giving you background information about the author, an introduction to the work, a graphical character map, critical commentaries, expanded glossaries, and a comprehensive index, all for you to use as an educational tool that will allow you to better understand *Paradise Lost*. This study guide was written with the assumption that you have read *Paradise Lost*. Reading a literary work doesn't mean that you immediately grasp the major themes and devices used by the author; this study guide will help supplement your reading to be sure you get all you can from Milton's *Paradise Lost*. CliffsNotes Review tests your comprehension of the original text and reinforces learning with questions and answers, practice projects, and more. For further information on John Milton and *Paradise Lost*, check out the CliffsNotes Resource Center.

CliffsNotes provides the following icons to highlight essential elements of particular interest:

Reveals the underlying themes in the work.

Helps you to more easily relate to or discover the depth of a character.

Uncovers elements such as setting, atmosphere, mystery, passion, violence, irony, symbolism, tragedy, foreshadowing, and satire.

Enables you to appreciate the nuances of words and phrases.

Don't Miss Our Web Site

Discover classic literature as well as modern-day treasures by visiting the CliffsNotes Web site at www.cliffsnotes.com. You can obtain a quick download of a CliffsNotes title, purchase a title in print form, browse our catalog, or view online samples.

You'll also find interactive tools that are fun and informative, links to interesting Web sites, tips, articles, and additional resources to help you, not only for literature, but for test prep, finance, careers, computers, and Internet too. See you at www.cliffsnotes.com!

LIFE AND BACKGROUND OF THE AUTHOR

The following abbreviated biography of John Milton is provided so that you might become more familiar with his life and the historical times that possibly influenced his writing. Read this Life and Background of the Author section and recall it when reading Milton's *Paradise Lost*, thinking of any thematic relationship between Milton's work and his life.

Early Years

John Milton was born in London on December 9, 1608. His parents were John Milton, Sr. and Sarah Jeffery, who lived in a prosperous neighborhood of merchants. John Milton, Sr. was a successful scrivener or copyist who also dabbled in real estate and was noted as a composer of liturgical church music. The Miltons were prosperous enough that eventually they owned a second house in the country.

Milton seems to have had a happy childhood. He spoke of his mother's "esteem, and the alms she bestowed." Of his father, Milton said that he "destined me from a child to the pursuits of Literature, . . . and had me daily instructed in the grammar school, and by other masters at home." Though the senior Milton came from a Catholic family, he was a Puritan himself. Milton's religion, therefore, was an outgrowth of family life and not something he chose at a later period in his maturity.

Education

Sometime, as early as age seven but perhaps later, Milton became a student at St. Paul's school, which was attached to the great cathedral of the same name. St. Paul's was a prestigious English public school—what would be called a "private school" in the U.S. Milton spent eight years as a "Pigeon at Paules," as the students were known, and came out a rather advanced scholar. He had studied the Trivium of Grammar, Rhetoric, and Logic and had probably been exposed to the Quadrivium of Mathematics, Geometry, Astronomy, and Music. He had also learned Latin well, was competent in Greek and Hebrew, had a smattering of French, and knew Italian well enough to write sonnets in it. The one language he did not study was English. Some of his language acquisition—Italian—came from private tutors hired by his father.

Also at St. Paul's, the young Milton made a friendship that was among the closest of his life with Charles Diodati. After leaving St. Paul's, the two young men would write each other in Latin. Through his friendship with Diodati, Milton came into contact with many of the foreign residents of London.

In 1625, Milton matriculated at Christ's College, Cambridge, intending to become a minister. Instead, Milton's facility with language and his abilities as a poet soon made the ministry a secondary consideration. Also, Milton was not pleased with the medieval scholastic curriculum that still existed at Christ's College. This displeasure caused him to become involved in frequent disputes, including some with his tutor William Chappell. In 1626, perhaps because of this dispute or perhaps because of some other minor infraction, Milton was "rusticated" or suspended for a brief period. Whatever the reason, Milton did not seem to mind the respite from Christ's, nor did the rustication impede his progression through the school in any significant way.

In March of 1629, Milton received his BA and three years later, in July 1632, completed work on his MA. In completing these degrees, Milton had already become an accomplished poet. His first significant effort was the Christmas ode "On the Morning of Christ's Nativity." Evidence also exists that he completed *L'Allegro* and *Il Penseroso* ("The Cheerful Man" and "The Pensive Man") while in college. These works had not achieved any notoriety for Milton, but they do demonstrate the genius that was within him.

Early Literary Work

After Milton's graduation, he did not consider the ministry. Instead, he began a six-year stay at his father's recently purchased country estate of Horton with the stated intention of becoming a poet. Milton made his move to Horton, a village of about 300 people, in 1632, saying that God had called him to be a poet. One of his first great works, *Comus, a Masque*, was written around this time.

In 1637, Milton's mother died, possibly of the plague. That same year, one of his Cambridge friends, Edward King, a young minister, was drowned in a boating accident. Classmates at Cambridge decided to create a memorial volume of poetry for their dead friend. Milton's poem, untitled in the volume but later called *Lycidas*, was the final poem, possibly because the editors recognized it as the artistic climax of the volume. Whatever the reasoning, the poem, signed simply J. M., has become one of the most recognized elegiac poems in English.

Influences Abroad

Having been through the years at Cambridge and six more at Horton, Milton took the Grand Tour, an extended visit to continental Europe. Such a tour was viewed as the culmination of the education of a cultivated young man. Milton as a true scholar and poet wanted more from this tour than just a good time away from home. He wanted to visit France and especially Italy. In Paris, in May of 1638, he met the famed Dutch legal scholar and theologian Hugo Grotius. Grotius' ideas on natural and positive law worked their way into many of Milton's political writings.

In Italy, Milton met a number of important men who would have influence on his writing. In Florence, he most likely met Galileo, who was under house arrest by the Inquisition for his heliocentric views of the solar system. Milton had a lifelong fascination with science and scientific discovery. Book VIII of *Paradise Lost* mentions the telescope and deals with planetary motions. Also in Italy, Milton attended an operatic performance in the company of Cardinal Francesco Barberino. The actual opera is not known but may have been one by Museo Clemente, who was popular at the time. Milton's own knowledge of and love for music shows up in much of his poetry, and, in some ways, *Paradise Lost* is operatic poetry. Finally, in Italy, Milton met Giovanni Batista, Marquis of Manso, who was the biographer of the great Italian epic poet, Torquato Tasso. Tasso's *Jerusalem Delivered* was obviously an influence on Milton's own epic poetry. To what extent Batista was also an influence is difficult to determine, but Milton did write the poem, *Mansus*, in his honor.

At this point in his journey, Milton planned to go to Greece but had to cut his tour short. Civil war was simmering in England; in addition, Milton learned that his old friend Charles Diodati had died. Late in 1638, Milton returned to London, where in 1639, he settled down as a schoolmaster for his nephews and other children from aristocratic families. For the first time in his life, Milton was on his own, earning his own way in the world.

Writing Career and Marriage

At this time, Milton began writing prose pamphlets on current church controversies. The political climate was charged as Charles I invaded Scotland, and the Long Parliament was convened. Milton wrote pamphlets entitled *Of Reformation*, *Of Prelatical Episcopacy*, and *Animadversions* in 1641, and *The Reason for Church Government* in 1642. For the young poet, the Puritan aspect of his work, at least in the public eye, began to take precedence over his poetry. Milton more and more sided with the idea that the church needed "purification" and that that sort of reform could not come from a church so closely connected to the king.

In 1642, the Civil War began, and its effects touched Milton directly. That same year, he married Mary Powell, daughter of a Royalist family from Oxford. A month after the marriage, Mary returned to Oxford to live with her family. The precise reasons for her leaving Milton are not known. Personal problems, political differences, or simple safety (Oxford was the headquarters for the Royalist army) may have motivated her. Milton's brother, Christopher, also announced as a Royalist at about this same time.

Whatever the reason for Mary Powell's desertion of Milton, he published the pamphlet *On the Doctrine and Discipline of Divorce* in 1643, followed by *On Education* and *Areopagitica* in 1644. Each of these works centered on the need for individual liberty. The ideas that Milton expressed in these writings are commonplace values today, but in the 1640s, they were so radical that Milton acquired the nickname, "Milton the divorcer."

Around 1645, Mary Powell returned to Milton. Once again, the reasons for her return are unclear. Charles I had lost the Battle of Naseby and any hope for military victory. The Powell family, avowed Royalists, were now in danger. They were ejected from their home in Oxford as Charles' power waned. Within a year of Mary's return to Milton, her entire family had moved in with the couple.

With the return of Mary and the arrival of her family, Milton was suddenly the head of a large household. His first collection of poetry, entitled *Poems*, was published in 1646. The volume included *Lycidas, Comus*, and "On the Morning of Christ's Nativity." In July, seven months after *Poems* was published, Milton's first daughter, Anne, was born. The marriage that had begun inauspiciously now seemed, if not perfect, at least sound.

Shortly after the reunion of Milton with his wife and the birth of his first child, both his father-in-law, Richard Powell, and his own father died. Milton was left with a moderate estate. He complained at this point that he was surrounded by "uncongenial people," a problem that was resolved a few months later when all the Powell relatives moved back to Oxford. Milton and his wife and daughter then moved into a smaller house in High Holborn. For the first time, the couple had a reasonably normal life and family. In 1648, a second daughter, Mary, was born.

The year 1649 marked a decisive change in Milton's life. Charles I was executed, with Milton probably in attendance. The murder of a king was shocking to the people of a country that had always lived under a monarchy and for whom the king had an aura of divinity. Milton attempted to justify the situation with his *Tenure of Kings and Magistrates*.

This pamphlet, along with Milton's other work for the Puritans, resulted in his being offered the position of Secretary for the Foreign Tongues. Milton now assumed full-time political office, corresponding with heads of states or their secretaries in Latin, the lingua franca of the day. Among other duties, he also responded to political attacks on the new Cromwellian government, particularly those attacking the philosophy and morality behind the violent overthrow of the monarchy. To this end, Milton wrote *Eikonoklastes* in response to *Eikon Basilike,* supposedly written by Charles the night before his execution, and *Defensio pro populo Anglicano* in response to Salmatius' *Defensio Regia*. During this period, Milton worked out of official lodgings in Scotland Yard.

Later Years

During 1652, Milton suffered a number of traumatic events. First, his eyesight, which had been growing weaker, gave out completely, probably because of glaucoma. By 1652, Milton was totally blind. Second, his young son, John, (b. 1651) died under mysterious circumstances. Third, his wife died from complications in giving birth to the Milton's third daughter, Deborah. And fourth, Pierre du Moulin published the pamphlet *Regii Sanguinis Clamor* (Outcry of the King's Blood), a pro-Charles pamphlet to which Milton was ordered to reply. Milton's reply was entitled *Defensio Secunda*, which was published in 1654. By that time, Andrew Marvell, Milton's friend and fellow poet, was working as his assistant. Milton was also allowed to cut back on his official labors and to use an amanuensis (akin to a secretary) as an aide.

Even with his personal and physical problems, Milton continued to write. His major personal project in the 1650s was *De Doctrina Christiana,* a work in which he tried to state formally all of his religious views. In 1656, he married Katherine Woodcock, who died two years later. He would marry for the third time in 1663 to Elizabeth Minshull, who became his nurse as his health declined in his later years.

With the death of Oliver Cromwell in 1658, Milton's political fortunes were reversed. As Royalists gained power, Milton went into hiding at the home of a friend. During this time, his *Defensio pro populo*

Anglicano and *Eikonoklastes* were publicly burned. Milton stayed in hiding until Parliament passed the Acts of Oblivion, pardoning most of those who had opposed Charles II. Even so, Parliament considered arresting Milton, an act which was carried out in October 1659. Fortunately for Milton, neither Charles nor his cohorts were especially bloodthirsty or vindictive, and Milton was released in December.

By the time of the actual restoration of the monarchy in 1660, Milton was hard at work on *Paradise Lost*. Milton had long considered writing a major work on the grand themes of Christianity. His familiarity with the *Iliad, Odyssey, Aeneid, The Divine Comedy,* and *Jerusalem Delivered* inclined him to the epic format. His preparations for the ministry as well as the natural bent of his Puritanism led him toward the subject of Man's fall. During much of the early 1660s, he worked on his epic and, in 1667, finally published *Paradise Lost*, an epic in ten books. He followed up his masterpiece with *Paradise Regained* and *Samson Agonistes* in 1671. Milton is thus one of a relatively small group of creative geniuses whose greatest works were written after they turned 50. The years of essay and pamphlet writing did not diminish his creative spark.

In 1674, Milton published the second edition of *Paradise Lost*, revising it to make a total of twelve books. Mostly he rearranged rather than rewrote. For example, he made what had been Book X into Books XI and XII. After the publication of the second edition, his health deteriorated, and on November 9, 1674, Milton died of complications from a gout attack. He was 66 years old. He was survived by his third wife and two of his daughters by Mary Powell. He was buried near his father's grave in Cripplegate. By 1700, *Paradise Lost* was recognized as one of the classics of English literature.

INTRODUCTION TO THE POEM

The following Introduction section is provided solely as an educational tool and is not meant to replace the experience of your reading the work. Read the Introduction and A Brief Synopsis to enhance your understanding of the work and to prepare yourself for the critical thinking that should take place whenever you read any work of fiction or nonfiction. Keep the List of Characters and Character Map at hand so that as you read the original literary work, if you encounter a character about whom you're uncertain, you can refer to the List of Characters and Character Map to refresh your memory.

Introduction

As early as his second year at Cambridge, John Milton had attempted to write an epic—a school exercise in Latin concerning the Gunpowder Plot. By his fourth year, he had expressed interest in composing an epic poem in English, possibly dealing with King Arthur. At this point in his life, Milton was certainly familiar with the classical Homeric epics of the *Iliad* and the *Odyssey*, as well as Virgil's *Aeneid*. Milton also knew Dante's *Divine Comedy*, which, while not technically an epic, has many epic characteristics. Finally, on his Grand Tour, Milton had met Giovanni Batista, the Marquis of Manso and biographer of Torquato Tasso, author of the epic *Jerusalem Delivered*.

From these sources, we can see the kind of poem that Milton had begun to envision. From Homer forward, the epic had been an extended narrative dealing with a hero or group of heroes attempting to achieve a specific goal. This goal frequently has to do with actions, events, or ideas that tend to define a culture either through history, values, or destiny, or, at times, all three. Any poem can be heroic, but the epic is separated from other heroic narratives through its magnitude and style. In simplest terms, epics are very long and written in a highly elevated style. The original Homeric epics, sometimes called *primary epics,* were orally recited by bards and involved ritualistic presentations.

Written, or *secondary,* epics made up for the lack of the bardic setting through heightened style and formal structures. These epics were always serious, involving important events, crucial to the culture of the author and his audience. Similarly, the poem dealt with public, even national, concerns rather than the private world of the artist. In terms of style, the epic was written in elevated, soaring language. For the Greeks and Romans, part of the elevated language was the use of hexameters. Moreover, the epic could contain a variety of forms such as narrative, lyric, elegy, satire, debate, and many others. The length of the poem allowed the author enormous leeway to present different types of poetry within the overall framework of the epic. The epic also was typified stylistically by beginning *in medias res* (in the middle of things) and using extended similes and metaphors, sometimes called *epic similes.* Generally, epics, before Milton, glorified warfare and heroism in warfare, focusing on heroes who distinguish themselves in battle. His

Milton came to the epic form with these ideas, but he also had his own epic in mind. Originally, Milton's notion seems to have been to follow the pattern of the *Iliad*, the *Odyssey*, and the *Aeneid* closely. His impulse to write on King Arthur, to create the *Arthuriad,* lends itself readily to the epic pattern. Over time though, Milton changed his mind about this epic. In the *Reason for Church Government,* he wonders "what king or knight before the conquest might be chosen in whom to lay the pattern of the Christian hero." The first answer to this query is obviously Arthur, but the second answer, upon reflection, is no one. By the Restoration, Milton's ideas of Christian hero and British epic were in flux.

The reasons for Milton's changed attitude toward his epic poem seem apparent. The changes in Milton's life are ample reasons for artistic changes. In the years between his Latin poems in which the epic theme of King Arthur is raised, Milton had seen his political fortunes rise and fall, had lived in hiding, had been imprisoned and freed with loss of prestige and reputation, had seen his hopes for a Christian nation fall apart, had gone blind, and had suffered through the deaths of two wives and two children. The young man filled with idealistic enthusiasm and nationalistic pride had been replaced by a man who now looked for a Christian hero who might embody "the better fortitude / Of Patience and Heroic Martyrdom," as he says in the prologue to Book IX of *Paradise Lost.* In the same prologue, he adds that he does not wish "to dissect / With long and tedious havoc fabl'd Knights / In Battles feign'd." None of such mainstays of earlier epics, he adds, give "Heroic name / To Person or to Poem."

Milton's whole concept of what an epic subject should be had changed. War, conquest, heroism in battle seemed like shams, and in Book VI of *Paradise Lost,* he wrote battle scenes that mock the epic convention. By the time he wrote his epic, Milton had found true heroism in obedience to God and in the patience to accept suffering without the loss of faith.

Exactly when Milton began *Paradise Lost* is open to question. Edward Phillips, Milton's nephew and early biographer, claimed to have heard parts of *Paradise Lost* as early as 1642. That Milton may have written poems and speeches that became a part of his epic well before the 1660s is not just possible but probable. In his Cambridge epic in Latin on the Gunpowder Plot, *In Quintum Novembris,* Satan appears as a character. In fact, in that early exercise, Satan calls a council of devils, and at the end of the poem, God laughs at the futility of the evildoers. Foreshadowings of *Paradise Lost* then occur as early as 1626. Further, in the Trinity manuscript of the 1640s, which contains a number of ideas for projects that Milton intended to pursue, there is an outline for a play called *Adam Unparadised*, containing a number of features that appear in *Paradise Lost.*

However, even though evidence exists that ideas for and sections of *Paradise Lost* existed well before the 1660s, strong evidence in the poem itself suggests that the main scenes and ideas of the epic occurred after 1660. That is, Milton had the idea for an epic poem while still in college. Over a period of close to 40 years, the plans for that epic developed and changed. Milton wrote many poems, songs, and speeches that seem now to be parts of *Paradise Lost.* But the one overriding fact remains that not until he was blind and finished with government work did Milton bring all that he had thought and worked on together into a complete epic structure.

In the end, Milton chose not to copy Homer and Virgil, but to create a Christian epic. His creation is still a work of great magnitude in an elevated style. Milton chose not to write in hexameters or in rhyme because of the natural limitations of English. Instead he wrote in unrhymed iambic pentameter, *or blank verse,* the most natural of poetic techniques in English. He also chose a new kind of heroism to magnify and ultimately created a new sort of epic—a Christian epic that focuses not on the military actions that create a nation but on the moral actions that create a world.

A Brief Synopsis

Each book of *Paradise Lost* is prefaced with an *argument,* or summary. These arguments were written by Milton and added because early readers had requested some sort of guide to the poem. Several of the books also begin with a prologue. The prologue to Book I states Milton's purpose: to tell about the fall of man and justify God's ways to man.

The epic begins traditionally *in medias res.* Satan and the other rebellious angels awake to find themselves in Hell on a lake of fire. Satan is lying beside Beelzebub. Satan raises himself from the lake and flies to the shore. He calls for the other angels to do the same, and they assemble by the lake. Satan tells them that all is not lost and tries to inspire his followers. Led by Mammon and Mulciber, the fallen angels build their capital and palace, Pandemonium. The highest ranking of the angels then assemble for a council.

In the council, Satan asks what the demons think should be the next move against God. Moloch argues for open warfare. Belial twists Moloch's arguments, proposing that nothing should be done. Mammon, the materialistic angel, argues that they do the best with what they have. Finally, Beelzebub, Satan's second in command, proposes that the angels try to get at God through his new creation, Man. Beelzebub's proposal, which is really Satan's proposal, is adopted, and Satan volunteers to find the new world and new creatures. He leaves at once, flying to the Gate of Hell. There, he meets his children, Sin and Death. Sin opens the gate for Satan who flies out into Chaos and Night. Sin and Death follow him. Finally, in the distance Satan sees Earth.

God watches Satan approach Earth and predicts his success in corrupting Man. Man has free will. But God omnisciently knows what will happen. God adds that Man can be saved through mercy and grace, but he must also accept the just punishment of death, unless someone takes on death for Man. The Son offers to become a man and suffer death in order to overcome it. The angels rejoice.

In the meantime, Satan, sitting on the edge of the Earth, cannot see the way to Man. Satan disguises himself as a cherub and flies to the sun to talk with the archangel, Uriel. Uriel shows Satan the way to Man.

Looking at Earth, Satan is taken with its beauty but quickly overcomes his sympathy to concentrate on what he must do. He sees Adam and Eve and is entranced with their beauty. As Satan listens to the pair, they talk about God's one commandment that they not eat from the Tree of Knowledge under penalty of death. Satan immediately begins to formulate a plan.

Uriel, on the sun, becomes suspicious of the cherub whose face shows changing emotions and goes to warn Gabriel. Gabriel says that he and his angels will capture any interlopers in the Garden, and late that night Ithuriel and Zephron capture Satan whispering in Eve's ear. The two angels bring Satan before Gabriel, who, with God's help, banishes the tempter from Earth.

When Eve awakes, she tells Adam of her troubling dream. Adam comforts her, reminding her that they are safe if they obey God. God decides to send the angel Raphael to warn Adam and Eve to be wary of Satan. Raphael goes to Earth where he eats with Adam and Eve. After the meal, Raphael tells Adam about the great rebellion in Heaven.

Raphael says that Lucifer (Satan) was jealous of the Son and through sophistic argument got his followers, about one third of the angels, to follow him to the North. There, only one of Satan's followers stood up against him—Abdiel, who returned to God.

Satan attacks God and the Heavenly Host, whose power has been limited by God. Nonetheless, God's forces have little difficulty in defeating the rebels. Michael splits Satan in half, which is humiliating, but not deadly, because Satan, as an angel, cannot die. After the first day of battle, the rebels construct a cannon and begin the second day's battle with some success. God's forces begin to pull up mountains and hurl them at the rebels, burying them and their cannons. God is amused at the presumption of the rebels but does not want the landscape destroyed. He sends the Son forth by himself in a chariot. The rebels are quickly herded into Hell.

Next, Raphael responds to Adam's questions about the creation of the world. The angel explains the day-by-day creation of the world in six days. Then, in an effort to keep the angel engaged in conversation, Adam asks about the motions of the heavenly bodies. Raphael explains that Adam should leave some questions to God's wisdom. Next, Adam describes his own creation, his introduction to Eden, and the creation of Eve. He describes how beautiful Eve is to him and the bliss of wedded love. Raphael gives Adam a final warning about Satan as he leaves.

Having been gone from Eden for eight days, Satan returns, sneaking in through a fountain near the Tree of Knowledge. He takes the form of a serpent to try to trick Man. When Adam and Eve awake, they argue over whether they should work together or alone. Eve finally convinces Adam to let her work by herself. Satan, in serpent's form, approaches Eve and, using clever but fallacious arguments, convinces her to eat the fruit of the Tree of Knowledge. After Eve eats, she reveals what she has done to Adam, who, unable to bear the thought of losing Eve, eats also. Having eaten the fruit, the two are overcome with lust and run to the woods to make love. When they awake, they are filled with shame and guilt. Each blames the other.

In Heaven, the angels are horrified that Man has fallen, but God assures them that He had foreknowledge of all that would happen. He sends the Son to Earth to pronounce judgment on the humans and the serpent. The Son goes to Earth and makes his judgments. He adds though, that through mercy, Adam and Eve and all humans may eventually be able to overcome death. In an act of pity, the Son clothes the two humans.

Sin and Death meanwhile have sensed an opportunity on Earth. They construct a huge causeway from Hell to Earth. On their way across, they meet Satan returning to Hell. They proceed to Earth while Satan enters Hell in disguise. Satan appears on his throne and announces what he has done. Expecting to hear the applause of all the fallen angels, he instead hears only hissing as he and all his followers are turned into snakes. When they eat the fruit of the Tree of Knowledge which appears before them, it turns to bitter ashes.

On Earth, Sin and Death see infinite opportunities. God, looking down on the two, says eventually they will be cast into Hell and sealed up. Adam and Eve lament, but Eve submissively asks Adam's forgiveness. He relents, his love overcoming his bitterness. She suggests suicide as a way to avoid the terrible curse on the world, but Adam says they must obey God.

God sends the angel, Michael, to take Adam and Eve out of Eden. Before doing so, Michael takes Adam to a hill and gives the human a vision of biblical history, ending with the birth of Jesus who will be the savior of Man. Adam rejoices. Adam and Eve together are led out of Eden. Behind them a flaming sword guards the entrance; ahead, they face a new life in a new world.

List of Characters

Primary Characters

God   The omnipotent, omniscient, and omnipresent creator of the universe. He is depicted as pure light by Milton and rules from an unmovable throne at the highest point in Heaven. God is the epitome of reason and intellect, qualities that often make him seem aloof and stern in the poem. His more merciful side is shown through his Son who is of course one of the Trinitarian aspects of God though not the same as God. God creates Man (Adam) and gives him free will, knowing that Man will fall. He also provides his Son, who becomes a man and suffers death, as the means to salvation for Man so that ultimately goodness will completely defeat evil.

Son   In the doctrine of the Trinity, the Godhead is made up of God the Father, God the Son, and God the Holy Spirit. Milton seems to make God the Son *not* co-eternal with the Father, though the theology here is not absolutely clear. The Son is presented to the angels well after the creation, and God's preferment of the Son causes Satan to rebel. The Son creates the Earth (he is referred to as God while doing so). The Son offers himself as a sacrifice to Death as a way to save Man after the Fall. The Son also defeats the rebellious angels and casts them into Hell. He shows the more merciful aspect of God.

Satan   Before his rebellion, he was known as Lucifer and was second only to God. His envy of the Son creates Sin, and in an incestuous relationship with his daughter, he produces the offspring, Death. His rebellion is easily crushed by the Son, and he is cast into Hell. His goal is to corrupt God's new creations, Man and Earth. He succeeds in bringing about the fall of Adam and Eve but is punished for the act. He can shift his shape and tempts Eve in the form of a serpent. He appears noble to Man but not in comparison to God.

Adam   The first human, created by God from the dust of Earth. He is part of God's creation after the rebellious angels have been defeated. At first Adam (and Eve) can talk with angels and seem destined to become like angels if they follow God's commands. Adam eats the fruit of the Tree of Knowledge because he cannot bear losing Eve. His inordinate desire for Eve is his downfall. He and Eve feud after the fall but are reconciled. They eventually go forth together to face the world and death.

Eve   Eve is the first woman, created by God from Adam's rib as a companion for him. She is more physically attractive than Adam, but not as strong physically or intellectually. She is seduced and tricked by Satan in the form of the serpent and eats the fruit of the Tree of Knowledge. She then tempts Adam whose love and desire for her is so strong that he eats the fruit rather than risk separation from Eve. Ultimately, Eve brings about reconciliation with Adam when she begs forgiveness from him. God promises that her seed will eventually bruise the head of the serpent, symbolically referring to Jesus overcoming Death and Satan.

Opposed to God

Death   Death is Satan's son and grandson, the result of an incestuous union between Satan and his daughter, Sin. Death has also had a relationship with Sin, producing the hellhounds that are at her side. Death is primarily an allegorical character. He is a shadowy figure with a ravenous appetite. He and Sin build a great bridge from Hell to Earth after Adam's and Eve's fall. God says that both Death and Sin will be sealed in Hell after Judgment Day.

Sin   The daughter of Satan who sprang from his head when he felt envy for the Son. She is beautiful to the waist but a hideous serpent beneath, with hellhounds that surround her and go in and out of her womb. The hounds are a product of her incestuous relationship with her son, Death, who was the product of a relationship with her father, Satan. In much of *Paradise Lost*, Sin is an allegorical character. She opens the Gate of Hell for Satan to leave. She and Death build a bridge to Earth and inhabit the world after Satan causes the Fall of Man. Eventually Sin and Death will be sealed in Hell.

Beelzebub   The devil second in rank to Satan. In the Bible, the name Beelzebub seems most likely to have been associated with the term "Lord of the Flies," the demon who drove flies away from sacrifices. Numerous theories exist but none are definitive or widely accepted. At best, the name Beelzebub exists in the Bible and is associated with Satan and evil. Milton's audience would have recognized Beelzebub as a demon, even if they probably knew little or nothing of his origins. He acts as Satan's mouthpiece in Book II.

Belial   In the Bible, Belial is a synonym for the devil or an adjective meaning wickedness or destruction. Milton presents him as an individual demon representing impurity. He argues cunningly and effectively for taking no action and is associated with "ignoble ease" (II, 227).

Mammon   In the Bible, Mammon is often presented as a king or demon who is the personification of wealth. In *Paradise Lost,* he is called the "least erected" of the fallen angels because he always has his eyes downward looking for gold or money. In the council, he proposes exploiting the wealth of Hell to create a comfortable existence rather than warring against God.

Moloch   Moloch was an idolatrous deity worshipped by some Israelites. The chief feature of his cult seems to have been child sacrifice. In *Paradise Lost,* he argues at the council for total war against God. He is neither subtle nor effective in his speech.

Mulciber   Fallen angel who is the chief architect for Pandemonium. The character seems to be derived from Hephaestus in Greek mythology.

Loyal to God

Michael   An archangel, one of the fiercest fighters in the battle between the rebellious angels and those loyal to God. Michael's name was a war cry of the good angels. In *Paradise Lost,* the fallen angels remember particularly the pain of Michael's sword. At the end of the epic, Michael reveals to Adam the biblical history of the world through the birth of Jesus. Michael also leads Adam and Eve out of Eden.

Raphael   One of the archangels. According to tradition Raphael was the angel of Man and was supposed to deal with Earth. Milton seems to follow that tradition since Raphael, often called the "affable archangel," is sent to Earth to warn Adam and to answer any questions Adam has. Many scholars fault Raphael's advice and find him complicit in the Fall of Man. The conversation between Raphael and Adam takes place in Books V—VIII.

Gabriel   In the Bible, the archangel Gabriel is the angel of mercy in contrast to Michael, the angel of justice. In the New Testament, Gabriel announces the coming of Jesus to Mary. In *Paradise Lost,* he is the angel who guards the gate of Eden. He captures Satan on his first attempt at corrupting Adam and Eve and sends him away.

Abdiel   Angel in Satan's host who opposes Satan's plan to rebel and returns to God. In the battle with the rebellious angels, Abdiel confronts Satan and pushes him backwards.

Ithuriel One of the angels who assist Gabriel in guarding Eden. Ithuriel and Zephron capture Satan whispering in Eve's ear.

Urania The name of Milton's muse. Classically, Urania is the Muse of Astronomy. Milton transforms her into Christian inspiration or the Holy Spirit.

Uriel One of the seven archangels. He is tricked by Satan disguised as a cherub. He realizes his mistake later and warns Gabriel that an interloper has entered the Garden of Eden.

Zephron One of the angels who assist Gabriel in guarding Eden. Zephron and Ithuriel discover Satan whispering in Eve's ear on his first attempt at corrupting Man.

Character Map

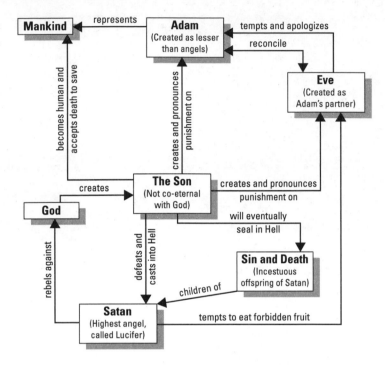

CRITICAL COMMENTARIES

The sections that follow provide great tools for supplementing your reading of *Paradise Lost*. First, in order to enhance your understanding of and enjoyment from reading, we provide quick summaries in case you have difficulty when you read the original literary work. Each summary is followed by commentary: literary devices, character analyses, themes, and so on. Keep in mind that the interpretations here are solely those of the author of this study guide and are used to jumpstart your thinking about the work. No single interpretation of a complex work like *Paradise Lost* is infallible or exhaustive, and you'll likely find that you interpret portions of the work differently from the author of this study guide. Read the original work and determine your own interpretations, referring to these Notes for supplemental meanings only.

Book I

Summary

Book I of *Paradise Lost* begins with a prologue in which Milton performs the traditional epic task of invoking the Muse and stating his purpose. He invokes the classical Muse, Urania, but also refers to her as the "Heav'nly Muse," implying the Christian nature of this work. He also says that the poem will deal with man's disobedience toward God and the results of that disobedience. He concludes the prologue by saying he will attempt to justify God's ways to men.

Following the prologue and invocation, Milton begins the epic with a description of Satan, lying on his back with the other rebellious angels, chained on a lake of fire. The poem thus commences in the middle of the story, as epics traditionally do. Satan, who had been Lucifer, the greatest angel, and his compatriots warred against God. They were defeated and cast from Heaven into the fires of Hell.

Lying on the lake, Satan is described as gigantic; he is compared to a Titan or the Leviathan. Next to Satan lies Beelzebub, Satan's second in command. Satan comments on how Beelzebub has been transformed for the worse by the punishment of God. Still he adds that it is his intention to continue the struggle against God, saying, "Better to reign in Hell than serve in Heaven" (263).

With effort, Satan is able to free himself from his chains and rise from the fire. He flies to a barren plain, followed by Beelzebub. From the plain, Satan calls the other fallen angels to join him, and one by one they rise from the lake and fly to their leader. As they come, Milton is able to list the major devils that now occupy Hell: Moloch, Chemos, Baalem, Ashtaroth, Astarte, Astoreth, Dagon, Rimmon, Osiris, Isis, Orus, Mammon, and Belial. Each devil is introduced in a formal cataloguing of demons. These fallen angels think that they have escaped from their chains through their own power, but Milton makes it clear that God alone has allowed them to do this.

This devil army is large and impressive but also aware of its recent ignominious defeat. Satan addresses them and rallies them. He tells them that they still have power and that their purpose will be to oppose God, adding, "War then, War / Open or understood, must be resolv'd" (661–62).

This speech inspires the devil host, and under Mammon's direction, they immediately begin work on a capital city for their Hellish empire. They find mineral resources in the mountains of Hell and quickly begin to construct a city. Under the direction of their architect, Mulciber, they construct a great tower that comes to symbolize the capital of Hell, Pandemonium. The devil army, flying this way and that, is compared to a great swarm of bees. When the work is done and the capital completed, they all assemble for the first great council.

Commentary

Milton begins Paradise Lost in the traditional epic manner with a prologue invoking the muse, in this case Urania, the Muse of Astronomy. He calls her the "Heav'nly Muse" (7) and says that he will sing "Of Man's First Disobedience" (1), the story of Adam and Eve and their fall from grace. As the prologue continues, it becomes apparent that this muse is more than just the classical Urania, but also a Christian muse who resides on Mt. Sinai, in fact the Holy Spirit. In these first lines, Milton thus draws on two traditions—the classical epic exemplified by Homer and Virgil and the Christian tradition embodied in the Bible as well as Dante's *Divine Comedy* and Edmund Spenser's *The Faerie Queene*.

Theme

Milton further emphasizes in the prologue that his theme will be *Man's* disobedience to God's will, implying not only Adam's disobedience, but all mankind from first to last. He does add that his subject will include the "greater Man" (4) who saved all others from the original disobedience. Moreover, his intention will be to "justify the ways of God to men" (26) through the aid of "Eternal Providence" (25). By "justify," Milton means more than simply to explain; he means that he will demonstrate that God's actions in regard to man are just. This goal suggests that Milton was not bothered by any sense of false modesty, an idea underscored by his statement that he will write in a high style and attempt a purpose never tried before. The one truly poignant line in this prologue is Milton's request of the muse, "What in me is dark / Illumine" (22—23), with its oblique reference to Milton's blindness, a subject he will return to more directly in the prologue that begins Book III. At no point in this prologue and invocation does Milton mention Satan, who, though he is the main character of the poem, is not the actual subject.

Following the invocation and prologue, Milton continues in the epic style by beginning *in medias res*, in the middle of things. Satan is first seen lying in the pit of Hell. That a great religious epic focuses on Satan, presents him first, and in many ways makes him the hero of the poem is certainly surprising and something of a risk on Milton's part. Milton does not want his audience to empathize with Satan, yet Satan is an attractive character, struggling against great odds. Of course, Milton's original audience more than his modern one would have been cognizant of the ironies involved in Satan's struggles and his comments concerning power. The power that Satan asserts and thinks he has is illusory. His power to act derives only from God, and his struggle against God has already been lost. To the modern audience, Satan may seem heroic as he struggles to make a Heaven of Hell, but the original audience knew, and Milton's lines confirm, that Satan's war with God had been lost absolutely before the poem begins. God grants Satan and the other devils the power to act for God's purposes, not theirs.

Also, at this point in the narrative, Satan is at his most attractive. He has just fallen from Heaven where he was the closest angel to God. He has not completely lost the angelic aura that was his in Heaven. As the poem progresses, the reader will see that Satan's character and appearance grow worse. Milton has carefully structured his work to show the consequences of Satan's actions.

The catalogue of demons that follows Satan's escape from the burning lake follows an epic pattern of listing heroes—although here the list is of villains. This particular catalogue seems almost an intentional parody of Homer's catalogue of Greek ships and heroes in Book II of the *Iliad*. The catalogue is a means for Milton to list many of the fallen angels as well as a way to account for many of the gods in pagan religions—they were originally among the angels who rebelled from God. Consequently, among these fallen angels are names such as Isis, Osiris, Baal, and others that the reader associates not with Christianity but with some ancient, pagan belief. Of the devils listed, the two most important are Beelzebub and Belial. (For a complete description of each devil, see the List of Characters.)

The final part of Book I is the construction of Pandemonium, the capital of Hell. A certain unintentional humor pervades this section of Book I as well as Mammon's argument in Book II. In both cases, a sense of civic pride seems to overcome the devils, and they act on the idea that "Hell is bad, but with a few improvements we can make it lots better, even attractive." In both Mammon and the hellish architect, Mulciber, the attitude of the mayor whose small town has been bypassed by the Interstate comes out. They both seem to think that with improvements Hell may be nice enough that others may want to relocate.

Style & Language

Milton's real goal here, though, is to establish Hell's capital, Pandemonium—a word which Milton himself coined from the Latin *pan* (all) and *demonium* (demons). Thus, the capital of Hell is literally the place of all demons. With the passage of time, the word came to mean any place of wild disorder, noise, and confusion. This idea is subtly emphasized with Milton's choice of Mulciber as the architect. Mulciber was another name for Hephaestus, the Greek God of the Forge, who was tossed from Olympus by a drunken Zeus. Mulciber is consequently a figure of some ridicule and not the most likely architect to build a lasting monument.

One other aspect of the construction of Pandemonium is worth consideration. Mammon and the other devils find mineral resources including gemstones in their search for building materials. This discovery of resources suggests that the Hell Milton has imagined is a multifaceted place. In the first scene, as Satan and the others lie chained on the burning lake, Hell seems totally a place of fiery torture and ugliness. The construction of Pandemonium shows that there is more to Hell. Geographic features such as a plain and hill, mineral resources such as gemstones, and even the possibility for beauty seem to exist in Hell. Other aspects of Hell will be brought forward in later books. All in all, Milton depicts a Hell that has more than one essence, or, at least in the opening books, seems to.

Glossary

justify (26) to show to be just, right, or in accord with reason; vindicate.

Ethereal (45) not earthly; heavenly; celestial.

Adamantine (48) of or like adamant; very hard; unbreakable.

Cherub (157) one of the winged heavenly beings that support the throne of God or act as guardian spirits.

Stygian (239) of or characteristic of the river Styx and the infernal regions; infernal or hellish.

puissant (632) powerful; strong.

Pandemonium (756) any place or scene of wild disorder, noise, or confusion; here, the capital of Hell.

Book II

Summary

At the start of Book II, Satan sits on his throne like a Middle Eastern potentate and addresses the assembled devils as to the course of action they should follow. Four of the devils speak—Moloch, Belial, Mammon, and Beelzebub—with Beelzebub being Satan's mouthpiece. Each speaker offers a different attitude concerning a solution for their Hellish predicament: Moloch proposes open warfare on Heaven; Belial proposes that they do nothing; Mammon argues that Hell may not be so bad, that it can be livable, even comfortable, if all the devils will work to improve it; and Beelzebub, Satan's mouthpiece, argues that the only way to secure revenge on Heaven is to corrupt God's newest creation: Man.

Beelzebub's (Satan's) plan carries the day, and Satan begins his journey up from Hell. At Hell's Gate, he is confronted by his daughter, Sin, a being whose upper torso is that of a beautiful woman but whose lower body is serpent-like. All around her waist are hellish, barking dogs. Across from Sin is her phantom-like son, Death.

Satan persuades Sin to open the gates, which she does, but she cannot close them again. Satan ventures forth into the realm of Chaos and Night, the companions that inhabit the void that separates Hell from Heaven. From Chaos, Satan learns that Earth is suspended from Heaven by a golden chain, and he immediately begins to make his way there. As Satan creates the path from Hell to Earth, Sin and Death follow him, constructing a broad highway.

Commentary

Book II divides into two large sections. The first is the debate among the devils concerning the proper course of action. The second section deals with Satan's voyage out of Hell with Sin and Death—the only extended allegory in *Paradise Lost*.

The council of demons that begins Book II recalls the many assemblies of heroes in both the *Iliad* and the *Aeneid*. Further the debates also seem based on the many meetings that Milton attended in his various official capacities. In his speech, each devil reveals both the characteristics of his personality and the type of evil he represents. For example, Moloch, the first to speak, is the unthinking man of action. Like Diomedes in the *Iliad*, he is not adept in speech, but he does know how to fight. He is for continued war and unconcerned about the consequences. But, moreover, the attitude toward violence exhibited by Moloch reveals a particular type of evil. In the *Inferno*, Dante had divided evils into three broad categories: sins of appetite, sins of will, and sins of reason. In the Renaissance, these categories still dominated much thought concerning the nature of evil. In Moloch, the reader sees a straightforward example of the evil that comes from the will. Unthinking violence is the result of lack of control of the will. And for Moloch, the "furious king" (VI, 357), violence defines his character.

In contrast to Moloch, Belial as a character type is a sophist, a man skilled in language, an intellectual who uses his powers to deceive and confuse. His basic argument is that the devils should do nothing. Belial wishes to avoid war and action, but he couches his arguments so skillfully that he answers possible objections from Moloch before those objections can be raised. He, in fact, rises to speak so quickly that the assembly is not able to respond to Moloch's idea. Belial also suggests the possibility that at some point God might allow the fallen angels back into Heaven, though these arguments seem specious at best and simply an excuse for cowardly inactivity. In terms of evil, Moloch uses reason for corrupt purposes. The use of reason for evil was theologically the greatest sin because reason separates man from animals. Belial's sophistry is not as corrupting as Beelzebub's and Satan's fraud will be, but it is still a sin of reason. Milton, in fact, introduces Belial as fair and handsome on the outside but "false and hollow" within (112). Milton makes the point about reason straightforwardly at the end of Belial's speech by referring to it as "words cloth'd in reason's garb" (226), as opposed to simply words of reason.

Belial's persuasive speech for nothing is followed by the practical, materialistic assessment of Mammon. Mammon sees the little picture. He finds no profit in war with God or in doing nothing. Hell, he argues can be made into a livable, even pleasurable place. In Heaven,

Mammon always looked down at the streets of gold. In Hell, he sees the gem and mineral wealth and thinks that Hell can be improved. In terms of sin, Mammon exhibits the sin of the appetite. Here the basic instinct of appetite controls the person. Mammon's desire for individual wealth controls his assessment of everything. The proverb that one cannot serve God and Mammon both easily translates to the idea that one cannot serve both God and one's appetite.

Finally, Beelzebub rises to speak—and he speaks for Satan. His argument to attack God by corrupting Man is Satan's argument. This idea is essentially a fait accompli; Satan has intended this plan all along and simply uses Beelzebub to present it. The entire council has been a sham, designed to rubber stamp Satan's design, a design that also allows Satan to leave Hell. Beelzebub's speech and actions are like those of Belial in that they pervert reason. But unlike Belial's arguments, Beelzebub's involve treachery against his fellow demons. All of the devils have involved themselves in treachery against God, but now Beelzebub and Satan compound this treachery by defrauding their own companions. The devils have seemingly been given a choice within a council, but in fact this seeming choice was illusion. They have been set up to do Satan's bidding. For many Renaissance thinkers, this type of treachery would have been considered Compound Fraud, the worst sin of all.

At this point, Satan begins his journey out of Hell to search for Earth and Man. The devils left behind explore Hell, finding various geographic areas including fire and ice, but also mountains and fields. Their exploratory activities along with their sports, songs, and games suggest another concept of Hell—Limbo, the part of Hell Catholicism recognized as reserved for virtuous pagans and unbaptised babies, a part of Hell that is Hell only in that those in it can never be in the presence of God. Limbo is an earthly paradise, and Milton seems to suggest that the fallen angels could have that for their punishment if they were content to accept their defeat by God.

Literary Device

As the devils explore Hell, Satan makes his way toward the gate out of Hell. This section of Book II begins the one extended allegory in *Paradise Lost*. An *allegory* is a literary work in which characters, plot, and action symbolize, in systematic fashion, ideas lying outside the work. While much of *Paradise Lost* deals with Christian ideas and theology, only in this section does Milton write in a true allegorical manner.

At the locked gate where he may exit Hell, Satan finds two guards: his daughter, Sin, and his grandson, Death. The way Sin and Death were created explains the nature of allegory. Sin was born when Satan, in Heaven, felt envy for Jesus. Sin sprang from Satan's head (symbolically his thoughts) just as Athena (wisdom) sprang from the head of Zeus. Death was born of the unnatural union between Satan and his daughter. Finally, adding to the general nastiness of the story, Death raped his own mother, Sin, creating the Cerberus-like hellhounds that gather around her waist.

The allegorical interpretation of this story is, in its simplest form, easy to follow. Satan's envy for Jesus was a sin, which becomes manifest in the character of his daughter, Sin. That is, the concept of sin in Satan's mind literally becomes Sin, a character. Sin, in conjunction with satanic evil, produces Death. Finally, Sin and Death together produce the hellhounds that will come to plague all mankind. The allegory here can be explored more deeply, but basically it explains, through characters and action, how sin and death entered the universe. Similarly, the fact that Sin opens the gate of Hell for Satan is also allegoric as is her inability to close it. Thus Satan, by leaving Hell, brings Sin and Death into the world.

Next Satan confronts the characters Chaos and Night. These two represent the great void that separates Earth from Hell. They are also part of the complex Renaissance cosmogony, but on the most basic level they represent the vast unorganized part of the universe away from Heaven and Earth. Hell lies on the other side of Chaos, and Night shows just how far removed Hell is, both figuratively and literally, from God.

Chaos and Night welcome Satan's attempt to cross the space between Heaven and Hell because they too lie outside the purview of Heaven. Satan becomes the pioneer who crosses the wilderness of Chaos and Night to find Earth, and in this effort he gains heroic stature. Within the allegory, however, he is simply charting the path for Sin and Death, since they follow him, building a broad highway. Once again the allegory is clear: Satan brings Sin and Death into the world where they will convey countless souls back across the broad highway to Hell. Also, the gate of Hell has been left open, and evils can now go from Hell to Earth at will.

Glossary

ambrosial (245)   of or fit for the gods; divine.

vassal / vassalage (253)   a subordinate, subject, servant, slave, etc.

Atlantean (305)   of or like Atlas; strong.

abyss (405)   *Theol.* the primeval void or chaos before the Creation.

Empyreal / Empyrean (430)   the highest heaven; among Christian poets, the abode of God.

lantskip (491)   landscape (a Dutch word whose form had not changed in English in Milton's time).

alchymy (516)   an early form of chemistry studied in the Middle Ages, whose chief aim was to change base metals into gold and to discover the elixir of perpetual youth. Milton uses the word in this instance in its meaning of "metal."

welkin (538)   the vault of heaven, the sky.

Styx, Acheron, Cocytus, Phlegethon (577)   the four rivers of Hell.

frith (919)   a narrow inlet or arm of the sea.

Book III

Summary

Book III opens with a prologue, often called "The Prologue to Light," that is addressed to the "holy light" of God and Heaven. In this prologue, Milton asks for God's light to shine inwardly so that he can reveal what no man has seen.

Following the prologue, Milton reveals God, the Son (Jesus), and the Heavenly Host in Heaven. God looks toward Earth and sees Satan approaching the home of Man. A council takes place in Heaven. This council is mainly made up of a discussion between God and the Son on how Man will respond to Satan's wiles and what the ultimate resolution will be. God says that Man will be corrupted by Satan's treachery but that the evil will redound to Satan himself.

Man's failure to resist temptation will, however, be Man's fault since God has provided Man with both the reason and the will to resist these temptations. Nevertheless, because the fall of Satan and the other rebellious angels is worse than Man's (the angels fell because of personal failures; Man will fall only because of outside forces), God will offer Man mercy through grace. God adds, however, that unless someone is willing to die for Man, Man will have to face death: Divine justice requires that penalty for Man's transgression. The Son says that he will suffer death but also overcome it and, through this sacrifice, redeem Man from Man's sin.

The scene of Book III now shifts from Heaven to Satan who has landed on the border between Earth and Chaos. From this seat in darkness, Satan sees a light and moves toward it. The light is a golden stairway leading to Heaven. From this new vantage point, Satan views the magnificence of the Earth and of the beautiful sun that illumines it. As Satan moves toward the sun, he sees the archangel Uriel and quickly transforms himself into a cherub. Satan deceives Uriel and asks where Man may be found. Uriel directs Satan toward Earth.

Commentary

Book III opens with a prologue as did Book I. This prologue is often called "The Prologue to Light" because it is addressed to the "holy light" of God and Heaven. Light here is associated with the eternal good and stands in contrast to the darkness associated with Hell and evil in Books I and II. The idea that stands out in the well-known "prologue to light" that opens Book III is how personal it is. Milton's blindness prevents him from seeing any light except the light of God, which illuminates the mind and which still allows him to be a poet. He makes references to the greatest classical epic poet, Homer (Maeonides), who according to tradition, was also blind, and to two mythic blind prophets, Tiresias and Phineas, who, even though blind, saw what others could not because of a gift from the gods.

Style & Language

Artistically then, Milton is able to place himself between the erudition of a classical "Invocation of Light" (as in Dante's *Paradiso*) and a personal, almost lyric, meditation on blindness. In the closing lines of this prologue, Milton brings the entire passage into focus as he asks for God's light to shine inwardly so that he can reveal what no man has seen. In this closing, he is able to transform the evil of his blindness into an intellectual and spiritual insight that surpasses anything possible by normal human sight. This notion of evil transformed to good is picked up thematically in the next section of Book III.

Character Insight

Milton took some risk in making God and the Son characters in *Paradise Lost*. The overriding problem was how to make a figure who is the embodiment of perfection, who is omnipotent, omniscient, and omnipresent, into a fictional character. Further, since the Son (Jesus) is, in traditional Christian belief, a part of the trinity and, therefore, a part of the godhead, how does he become a separate character from God? Milton dealt with the first problem in his characterization of God, a characterization that has received a fair amount of criticism. As to the second problem, Milton was not a Trinitarian. He did not accept that God and Jesus were co-eternal, and he believed that Jesus was, in the strict hierarchy of the universe, imperceptibly to man, lower than God. Therefore, he was able to treat the Son as a separate and distinct character from God, even as the Son has powers equal to God and is sometimes referred to as God.

In the second section of Book III, the council in Heaven, Milton presents an obvious contrast with the council of the demons in Hell in

Book II. Here the reader sees clearly that God is in control of all, including Satan. Further, in their speeches, God and the Son provide the arguments that begin Milton's justification of the ways of God to man.

Milton runs a great artistic risk in introducing God as a character because God must then make the theological arguments that are introduced. God must explain the creation of Man, Man's temptation by Satan, and Man's fall. But further, God must clearly explain why his foreknowledge of these events in no way means that Man's fall is predestined in the sense that God causes it. Instead, he must show that the fall results from the failure of Man to use the gifts and abilities God has granted to him. Then God must convince the reader that Man deserves punishment for the fall, including eternal death if no one will step forward to accept death in Man's place.

Theme

God's argument is essentially that Man has free will, that Man has the power to resist temptation, but that Man will give in to temptation because he does not use his powers. God's foreknowledge that Man will fall in no way indicates predestination. God simply knows what Man will do; God does not cause Man to do it. Since Man falls away from God because of Man's weakness, Man deserves punishment, even death. However, because Man was tempted to the fall by Satan, Man also deserves a chance for redemption and salvation. The entire argument is scholastic, even pedantic, and in making it, God sounds more like a Dickensian schoolmaster than a magnanimous and loving father, and at this point, God's argument seems weakest. He created Man, he allows Satan to tempt Man, and then he blames Man for it. Man can be saved, but he must die. Divine Justice requires the punishment even as Divine Love offers salvation. The only way to resolve the quandary is for someone to take death on for Man.

Intellectually the argument may be sound, but for many readers, God seems to be an administrator more interested in following the written down procedures rather than looking at the specific situation. Still, for Milton's purpose, God's view must be presented in a clear and closely reasoned argument. Who better then to present God's argument then than God himself? Probably no author can create God as a character and not make him less than the sense of God in a reader's mind. For his purpose of justifying God's ways to man, Milton does what he has to do. The questionable depiction of God is somewhat redeemed by Milton's representation of the Son (called "the Son" since Jesus, in the poem's time, has not yet been born into the world). The Son sees a solution to the problem and steps forward willingly, accepting death in order to overcome it and save Man. The Son seems generous and loving, and through the Son, the reader is able to see God's love and concern for Man and move beyond the legalistic debate points of God's opening argument. Finally, in the hymn the Heavenly Host sings in adoration of the Son, the reader finally sees something of the glory of Heaven that, up until this point, Milton has ignored.

Character Insight

This passage also highlights the contrast between the Son and Satan. Satan asked his council which demon would leave Hell to find Earth and corrupt Man. When no demon volunteered, Satan undertook the task himself. The Son takes on the opposite and more onerous task of becoming man, going to Earth, and suffering death in order to save Man. In motive, spirit, and action, Satan and the Son are almost direct opposites.

In the final section of Book III, Milton turns his attention back to Satan, who sits between Chaos and Earth contemplating his next move. Here Milton interrupts the flow of the narrative to describe a future Limbo of Vanity or Paradise of Fools that will occupy the area where Satan sits. This description is Milton's digressive view of the future and not something that Satan imagines. Over the years, many commentators have questioned the positioning and effect of this passage. Milton stops the flow of his story and argument to describe such foolish sinners as those who built the Tower of Babel and the philosopher Empedocles, who thought to prove himself immortal by jumping into a volcano only to have the volcano prove the opposite by spewing his dead body back out. To this group of foolish sinners, Milton adds a group of monks, friars, and priests in an obvious satire on Catholicism and such beliefs as Limbo, which Protestantism had rejected. It is difficult to defend Milton's positioning of this digressive passage at this place in the poem.

Theme

The last scene of Book III shows Satan as a shape-shifter. He assumes the appearance of a cherub, one of a lesser order of angels, to speak with the archangel, Uriel, on the sun. (The sun itself provides a fitting end to Book III since the book opened with the "Invocation to Light" and will now close with the sun shining over the Earth.) Satan's guise as a cherub graphically demonstrates two thematic ideas that will continue to recur in the poem. First, Satan will, in varying ways, be diminished from the magnificent being he first appears to be in Book I. The cherub disguise, one in which he appears as a much smaller and less significant angel than he once was, is the first of several images that convey this idea. Second, Uriel does not recognize Satan because the disguise exemplifies hypocrisy. Milton says that hypocrisy is the one sin that angels cannot recognize. Only omniscient God can see hypocrisy. In later books, Satan will not always be able to use hypocrisy to hide his identity. Here though, in cherub form, Satan gets from Uriel the information he needs to find Adam, Eve, and the Garden.

Glossary

glozing (93)   [Obs.] to fawn or flatter. Used by Milton to describe Satan's lies.

foreknowledge (118)   knowledge of something before it happens or exists; prescience.

incarnate (315)   endowed with a body, esp. a human body; in bodily form. The Son will become *incarnate* to save Man.

Fiend (430)   here, Satan.

Chaos (421)   the disorder of formless matter and infinite space, supposed to have existed before the ordered universe Milton personifies.

wicket (484)   a small door or gate, esp. one set in or near a larger door or gate. Used by Milton for Heaven's Gate.

Limbo (495)   in some Christian theologies, the eternal abode or state, neither heaven nor hell, of the souls of infants or others dying in original sin but free of grievous personal sin, or, those dying before the coming of Christ; the temporary abode or state of all holy souls after death.

Seraph, Seraphim (667)   any of the highest order of angels.

bower (734)   a place enclosed by overhanging boughs of trees or by vines on a trellis; arbor.

Book IV

Summary

Book IV opens with a soliloquy by Satan. As he looks from Mt. Niphrates toward Earth, he thinks on all that he has done and the options open to him. He concludes that his only recourse is evil, and from now on, all his efforts will be to, if not destroy, at least divide God's kingdom. He will carve out a place where he can reign. As Satan considers these ideas, his face changes, revealing his conflicting emotions. On the sun, Uriel notices these emotions and realizes that the cherub cannot be an angel because the minds of angels are always at peace. Uriel sets off to find Gabriel to inform him of the being in the guise of a cherub.

Satan meanwhile moves toward Earth and Paradise—the Garden of Eden. The Garden is on top of a mountain offering only limited and difficult access. Satan gains access to the Garden by leaping the wall like an animal or thief. Once there, he sits in the Tree of Life in the form of a cormorant, a bird of prey. From this vantage, Satan is impressed with the beauty of Eden and the pure air he breathes. Even so, he begins to plot the destruction of God's new creation. Satan sees Man for the first time as Adam and Eve walk through the Garden. While Satan admires the pair and admits that he could love them, he adds that he, nonetheless, means to destroy them and their peaceful life in Paradise.

Uriel arrives at the gate of Eden to inform Gabriel about the interloper in the form of a cherub. Gabriel responds that no one unauthorized has come to the gate. He adds that if someone has managed to come into the Garden by crossing the wall, he and his assistants will find them by morning.

In Eden, Adam and Eve prepare for bed. Adam reminds Eve that they must work tending the Garden, keeping nature within bounds. He also reminds her of their one proscription from God—not to eat from the Tree of Knowledge. Then, hand in hand, they enter their bower for bed, where they enjoy the sexual love of husband and wife and fall asleep.

Outside Gabriel assembles his troops and sends them to search Eden for the interloper. Zephron and Ithuriel find Satan in the bower of Adam and Eve. The devil, "squat like a toad," is beside Eve, whispering in her ear, trying to produce nightmares. The two angels bring him out to face Gabriel, who questions Satan about his motives for entering Eden. Satan craftily replies that those in Hell seek a better place. He had come to scout out Earth but not to do evil. After further discussion, Gabriel accuses Satan of shifting arguments and threatens to drag the demon back to Hell in chains if he does not immediately return on his own. In anger, Satan rises to his full height, still magnificent even though diminished. Gabriel and his troops prepare for battle, but God cuts the conflict short by holding up a pair of golden scales in the sky. Both Satan and Gabriel recognize the symbol and the power behind it. Satan especially realizes that he cannot overcome God's will and flies away into the night, muttering to himself.

Commentary

Literary Device

In the opening section of Book IV, Satan talks to himself, and for the first time, the reader is allowed to hear the inner workings of the demon's mind. This opening passage is very similar to a soliloquy in a Shakespearean drama, and Milton uses it for the same effect. Traditionally, the soliloquy was a speech given by a character alone on the stage in which his innermost thoughts are revealed. Thoughts expressed in a soliloquy were accepted as true because the speaker has no motive to lie to himself. The soliloquy then provided the dramatist a means to explain the precise motivations and mental processes of a character. Milton uses Satan's opening soliloquy in Book IV for the same purpose.

Character Insight

In his soliloquy, Satan reveals himself as a complex and conflicted individual. He literally argues with himself, attempting first to blame his misery on God but then admitting that his own free will caused him to rebel. He finally concludes that wherever he is, Hell is there also; in fact, he himself is Hell. In this conclusion, Satan develops a new definition of Hell as a spiritual state of estrangement from God. Yet even as he reaches this conclusion, Satan refuses the idea of reconcilement with God, instead declaring that evil will become his good and through evil he will continue to war with God. The self-portrait that Satan creates in this soliloquy is very close to the modern notion of the anti-hero—a character estranged and alienated who nonetheless will not alter his own attitudes or actions to achieve redemption from or reintegration with society at large.

As Satan debates with himself, he is still in the form of a cherub. The different guises and shapes that Satan assumes become a revealing pattern in the work. In Book I, Satan appeared almost as he had in Heaven—a majestic being. Here at the start of Book IV, he is in the form of a cherub, a much lesser angel. Next, when he leaps the wall into Eden, he sits in the Tree of Life as a cormorant, a large ravening sea bird that symbolizes greed. As he explores Eden and observes Adam and Eve, he takes the forms of a lion and a tiger. Finally, when he is captured whispering in Eve's ear, he is described as "squat like a toad." The devolution or degeneration of Satan in these different shapes is readily apparent. He moves from archangel to lesser angel, from angel to bird—a creature that still flies. Next he is a lion and a tiger—dangerous beasts, feared by Man but nonetheless beautiful and noble in bearing. Finally, he is described as being like the low and homely frog. The idea that evil corrupts and diminishes is made graphic in Satan's various guises.

Milton goes even further with images of shape shifting. When Zephron captures Satan squatting like a toad, Satan immediately assumes his actual shape. Yet, at this point, his real appearance is so changed that Zephron does not recognize him. The animal forms that Satan has assumed symbolize the actual degradation that is taking place in both Satan's physical appearance and moral character. Milton makes the point that evil is a destructive and degenerative force almost palpable as he describes the different physical changes that Satan goes through.

While Satan's soliloquy and shape shifting are important, the most memorable part of Book IV is Milton's description of Eden and the introduction of Adam and Eve. Eden is described as a garden on a plateau-like mountain. It is surrounded by a wall and has only one entrance, guarded by angels. Milton depicts the Garden itself in lush, sensuous detail with the two trees—the Tree of Life and the Tree of Knowledge—singled out. The image of Satan sitting in the Tree of Life in the shape of a cormorant presages the entrance of Death into Paradise.

A significant aspect of Milton's description of the Garden is the role that Adam and Eve have there. Their duty is to tend Eden, to keep nature from running wild. The implication here is that Man brings order to nature. Nature is beautiful in itself but also without control. Left alone, the beauty of nature can be lost in weeds, unchecked growth, and decay. Eve mentions how difficult it is for the two humans to do all that is necessary. Some commentators see the struggle between Man and nature as one of the basic themes in all literature. Nature represents the Dionysian side of the universe, emotional, unrestrained, without law, while Man represents the Apollonian side, moral, restrained, lawfully structured. Nature runs rampant: Man civilizes. Milton's description of the Garden and Adam's and Eve's duties within it bring this Dionysian / Apollonian contrast into play. Satan's entrance into the Garden shows that both the natural and civilized aspects of the world can be corrupted by evil.

Milton also emphasizes the physical nature of the love between Adam and Eve. Some Puritans felt that sex was part of the fall of man, but Milton literally sings the praises of wedded love, offering an Epithalamion or wedding song at line 743. Milton does emphasize the bliss of wedded love as opposed to animalistic passion, however.

Milton also provides insight into the characters of Adam and Eve. At line 411, Adam reminds Eve of the one charge God has given them—not to eat from the Tree of the Knowledge of Good and Evil. While this short speech reminds the reader of what will happen when Satan gains access to Adam and Eve, it also hints that Adam may think too much about God's proscription concerning the Tree, since there is no particular reason for him to bring the warning concerning the tree up at this point in the poem.

The introduction of Eve even more obviously reveals her character and points to the future. Eve describes how she fell in love with her own image when she first awoke and looked in the water. Only the voice of God prevented this narcissistic event from happening. God turned Eve from herself and toward Adam. The suggestion here is that Eve's vanity can easily get her into trouble. Eve's weakness is further indicated in her relationship with Adam. Adam is superior in strength and intellect while Eve is the ideal companion in her perfect femininity. This relationship is sexist by modern standards but reflects the beliefs of Puritan England as well as most of the rest of the world at the time. Even so, Eve's dependence on Adam suggests that she could be in trouble if she has to make serious decisions without Adam's aid. Eve's vanity and feminine weakness in conjunction with Adam's warning about the Tree of Knowledge are a clear foreshadowing that Eve will eventually yield to temptation.

The final scene of Book IV, as Satan confronts Gabriel and a small phalanx of angels, has received much criticism from commentators. Milton's description of Satan as he confronts the angels emphasizes the devil's power and magnificence even in his corrupted state. The scene seems to call for a battle, but Milton instead produces a *deus ex machina* in the form of a golden scale in the heavens. The suggestion that Satan has been weighed and found wanting causes the great demon immediately to fly away. The intense drama of the moment fizzles with the image of the scale and Satan's inglorious departure. Of course, Milton's point is that the only power of Satan or the angels comes from God, and, at this moment, God chooses to exert his own power symbolically. In terms of drama, the ending of Book IV may be unsatisfying, but in terms of theology, it reminds the reader of where the real power in the universe resides.

Glossary

Apocalypse (2)   any of various Jewish and Christian pseudonymous writings (*c.* 200 B.C.–*c.* A.D. 300) depicting symbolically the ultimate destruction of evil and triumph of good.

visage (116)   the face, with reference to the expression; countenance.

irriguous (255)   moist, well-watered.

nuptial (339)   of marriage or a wedding.

Purlieu (404)   orig., an outlying part of a forest.

impregn (500)   impregnate.

arede (962)   advise.

phalanx (979)   an ancient military formation of infantry in close, deep ranks with shields overlapping and spears extended.

Book V

Summary

As Adam and Eve wake up, Eve reports a troublesome dream in which an angel-like being tempted her to eat fruit from the Tree of Knowledge. After first hesitating, she ate from the fruit the being held up to her. Adam is troubled by Eve's dream but, after discussing possible sources of the images with her, concludes that the dream is not necessarily evil, that Eve is too pure to do evil, and that the events of the dream will not actually come true.

As Adam and Eve turn to their daily obligations, God and the seraphim Raphael look down on them from Heaven. God says that he pities the humans because he knows they will yield to temptation. Still, he sends Raphael to Eden to remind Adam that he and Eve have free will, that Satan intends to tempt them to evil, and that they have the power to resist Satan, as well as the free will to give in.

In the Garden, Raphael explains to Adam that eventually he and Eve may be able to attain a purer state and be like the angels. He adds the caveat, though, that Adam must remain obedient to God. When Adam questions whether he can actually be disobedient, Raphael reminds Adam that God has given the humans free will; Adam's obedience to God is up to him. Adam is sure that he could never disobey God, but some questions have entered his mind. He asks Raphael to tell him the story of the rebellious angels.

Here Raphael begins the story of the great rebellion in Heaven: When God introduced his newly begotten Son, destined to become King of the Angels in Heaven, the angels rejoiced. However, Satan (Raphael explains that his former name, Lucifer, is no longer used) was not pleased. As the principal archangel, Satan had seen himself as second only to God and had no wish to acknowledge the Son as his superior. Satan and his second in command roused his legions against the Son and, through their cunning arguments, convinced a third of the angels to follow them to the North. God and the Son were aware of Satan's actions and amused at his presumption. The Son indicated that the rebellion would simply allow him to reveal his power by overcoming the rebels.

In the North, Satan addressed his followers, attempting to harden their hearts totally against God. Only one of Satan's followers, Abdiel, opposed him. Satan tried to sway Abdiel and, when he failed, told Abdiel to leave and inform God that Satan and his hosts would rule themselves and test their power against God's. Abdiel left, not because of Satan's order, but because he was faithful to God. He alone of Satan's followers remained loyal to God.

Commentary

Literary Device

Eve's dream at the start of Book V is an obvious foreshadowing of the actual temptation scene in Book IX. This foreshadowing, however, is also ironic in that the reader already knows that Eve—and Adam—will yield to the temptation of Satan. Thus, rather than being simply an instance of foreshadowing, Eve's dream is confirmation and emphasis on what the reader knows must and will happen. Further, by bringing up the dream at this point in the text, Milton makes the reader analogous to God. Both God and the reader know that Adam and Eve will fall, but neither the reader nor God is the cause of that fall. Consequently, when Adam tells Eve that the dream will not come true, that it is bred of fear rather than reason, the reader, once again like God, knows that Adam is wrong but can do nothing to help him.

The set up of Eve's dream segues nicely into another brief discussion of free will—this time between God and Raphael. Here God does what the reader cannot: He sends a warning to Adam, reminding him that Satan will try to tempt Mankind to disobedience and that Adam's and Eve's free will *can* allow them to give in to that temptation. God's warning stops just short of telling Adam exactly what will happen.

At times Milton seems almost obsessive on his insistence of the idea of free will. Certainly, the idea that Adam has free will is central to Milton's theology, and, like a teacher with a student before a test, Milton wants to drive the point home to the reader. Adam has free will. God is omniscient. He knows Adam will fall, but he does not cause the fall. In fact, God actively tries to thwart the fall. But God, like the reader, ultimately knows that nothing can change the outcome for Adam and Eve.

An interesting sidebar to Raphael's visit to Adam is the fact that the angel can eat, in fact needs to eat, although human food is not his normal fare. The point of the scene is to show Adam that through obedience to God, he may rise to a higher spiritual level and become like the angels. However, the force of the scene comes from the gusto with which Raphael partakes of Eve's meal. For a modern reader, Raphael is reminiscent of John Travolta's portrayal of the angel Michael in the movie *Michael*. Raphael seems to enjoy human food a little too much. Beyond this unintentional humor though, Milton uses Raphael's appetite for a brief discourse on how all the elements of the universe pass from one to the other in a large circle. The food that Man eats nourishes not only his physical body but also sustains his reason, Man's highest faculty. In angels, a more sublime food produces the even higher faculty of intuition so that angels know with an immediacy that Man, relying on reason, cannot.

Theme

Raphael then goes a step further, showing the hierarchical relationship of all nature. He takes the four basic elements—earth, water, air, and fire—and shows that earth feeds water (the sea). Together, earth and the sea feed air, which, in turn, feeds the eternal fire. The point of this hierarchy, which permeated much Renaissance thought, is to demonstrate that everything tends toward its higher calling. In Man, reason is the highest faculty, and Man (Adam) must use his reason as his highest defense if confronted with temptation. Raphael's discussion and description of these hierarchies then is part of his warning to Adam.

Raphael next turns to the rebellion in Heaven of Satan and his followers. Before he describes the actual events of the rebellion, Raphael tells Adam that humans cannot fully comprehend the spiritual or angelic nature of such events. Raphael, therefore, will tell the story using earthly counterparts to Heavenly notions. In a sense, Raphael explains one of the functions of art, to put difficult concepts into understandable form through metaphor. He will tell Adam what the war in Heaven was like because Adam will be unable to understand the real nature of the conflict.

The story Raphael tells preceded the opening of *Paradise Lost*. Because of epic tradition, Milton opened his story in the middle of things, *in medias res*. So now, Milton uses Raphael's story as a means to go back and relate the events that led up to the opening of Book I. Raphael's story, which covers Books V and VI, is a type of flashback, a story that precedes the main action of the epic.

Raphael says that the rebellion began when God presented his newly "begotten" Son to the angels as their new ruler. Many commentators have been troubled by Milton's use of the word "begotten" since it suggests that the Son was "born" to God and thus denies the doctrine of the Trinity. However, Milton also uses the term "anointed" as a synonym for "begotten," and so the generally accepted meaning for the passage is that the Son is now begotten or anointed as the Messiah or King of Heaven to rule over the angels.

The rest of Raphael's description of the rebellion gives the lie to Satan's description of the rebellion in Book I. Satan was not heroic in his opposition to God; instead he sneaked away in the night. Further, he convinced other angels to follow him with sophistic arguments and the magnificence of his appearance in Heaven. The real hero of the last part of Book V is Abdiel who follows his own beliefs and challenges Satan in front of all the Devils' hosts. Abdiel cannot be swayed by Satan's arguments and taunts and heroically deserts Satan. Abdiel is the only one of Satan's hosts who has the fortitude and moral character to oppose the mighty archangel. Milton here gives the reader a direct contrast between pomp without substance (Satan) and substance without pomp (Abdiel).

Abdiel also stands as an example for both Satan and for Adam and Eve. That is, Abdiel responds appropriately when confronted with temptation. Had Satan resisted his own envious thoughts, he would not have rebelled. Had the other angels been like Abdiel, they would not have followed Satan; they would have remained true to God. If Adam and Eve had been like Abdiel, they would not have eaten from the Tree of Knowledge. Abdiel shows that free will exists and can be used.

Glossary

wont (32)   accustomed: used predicatively.

orison (145)   a prayer.

Prime (170)   a part of the Divine Office orig. assigned to the first hour of daylight; Milton uses Prime in the sense of dawn, the first hour of daylight.

quaternion (181)   a set of four.

Hail (385)   a greeting, used by Raphael specifically to suggest the same greeting the angel of the Annunciation will used when he comes to Mary in Luke i, 28.

progeny (503)   children, descendants, or offspring.

ineffable (734)   too overwhelming to be expressed or described in words.

Book VI

Summary

Book VI continues Raphael's account of the war in Heaven and opens as Abdiel makes his way back to God from Satan's hosts in the North. The other angels welcome Abdiel and take him before God, who praises the loyal angel for standing for truth even though none stood with him. God then appoints Michael and Gabriel to lead the Heavenly forces against Satan's army. However, God limits the number of the Heavenly force and its power to equal that of Satan's hosts.

The battles lasts two days. On the first day, the angels easily beat the rebellious angels back; on the second day, under the assault of a cannon that the demons have built, the angels' victory is not so easy. In response to the cannon fire, the Heavenly hosts grab mountains, hills, and boulders and pelt the rebels, literally burying them and their cannon. The rebels dig out and begin to respond in kind, and the air is soon filled with the landscape. At this point, God, fearing for the physical safety of Heaven (he knows that Satan is no real threat to his power, but the rebels are literally uprooting the landscape), calls forth the Son, who attacks the rebels single-handedly in his chariot and easily herds them into a gap that opens into Hell. Afraid to go forward or back, the rebels are eventually forced through the gap into Hell.

Raphael concludes his narrative and tells Adam that Satan now envies Man's position and will try to tempt the two humans into disobedience. Raphael reminds Adam of the fate of the rebellious angels and warns him not to yield to temptation.

Commentary

In Book VI, Milton presents his description of epic warfare. He follows many of the conventions of the great classic epics, such as the *Iliad* and the *Aeneid*, by giving graphic descriptions of battles and wounds, highlighting the boasting give and take in individual battles, and developing massive scenes of chaotic violence. However, Milton goes beyond his classical models and, in a sense, mocks the nature of the warfare he describes. The reasons that lie behind this sense of mockery in Book VI have been frequently discussed and disputed by critics and commentators. The general sense of those who see a kind of mocking humor in the battle scenes is that Milton was dealing with two difficulties. First, the combat in Heaven is between combatants who cannot be killed, and second, there is no doubt as to the outcome of the battle.

To begin with, in Book V, Raphael has told Adam that the description of the war must of necessity be metaphoric. That is, the human mind cannot grasp the real nature of war in Heaven, so Raphael must use a comparative, metaphoric technique to make the event understandable to Adam. From the start of Raphael's description then, the idea that immortal angels with God-like powers would need armor, swords, even a special cannon, is ludicrous. The angels, both loyal and rebellious, are so powerful that such weapons would be, at best, superfluous and, at worst, bothersome. So the entire nature of the warfare that Raphael lays out must be understood as only a means to allow Adam's human reason to gain some idea of what actually happened in Heaven.

An alternative view to the angels' use of weapons suggests that Milton was attempting to present all of the types of warfare known, from the swords and spears of Homeric legend, through medieval armor to the gunpowder and cannons of the Renaissance and Restoration. While this reason for the weapons may be valid, it has no bearing on the serio-comic tone of the warfare in general, a tone that results from Raphael's inability to accurately express Heavenly fighting.

Style & Language

In relating his warfare metaphor, Raphael, either wittingly or unwittingly, creates the feel of a mock-epic rather than true dramatic epic. The individual encounters have a cartoonish aspect about them. Abdiel, whose heroism in standing up to Satan receives deserved praise from God, first confronts Satan and knocks him backwards. Next, Michael splits him down the middle. In the *Iliad*, such a wound would be the end of the warrior. But, in *Paradise Lost*, Satan cannot be killed so the wound, like wounds in cartoons, heals. The reader sees Satan split open but knows he will be back. Moloch is similarly chased screaming from the field in ignominious fashion. Everywhere, demons are humiliated, while the angels, limited in numbers and power by God, hardly break ranks. Even if Milton's goal in this scene is not exactly comedy, it is to demonstrate through the one-sidedness of the fight that the rebels have no real power over God. Dramatic tension cannot be produced when the outcome is preordained.

The semi-serious tone of Book VI continues in the description of the second day of battle. Satan has foolishly convinced his troops to build a cannon to continue the fight. The foolishness comes from the notion that a different weapon will be more effective than the first ones. If angels cannot be killed by swords, neither can they be killed by a cannon. The futility of their plans is lost on Satan and his cohorts. Some comedy does ensue when the demons fire their cannon because several rows of angels are bowled over by the cannonball. This result produces mockery and gloating by Satan and Belial. Their gloating, unlike the deep laughter of God at the rebels' presumption, however, is false optimism. Their gloating is simply prelude to the angels' response, which is a barrage of boulders, hills, and mountains that literally bury the rebels and their cannon, another cartoon-like image. This image is followed by another of the same sort as the rebels dig their way out and begin to lob parts of the landscape back at the angels. This depiction of the hills and mountains flying through the air and landing on unsuspecting angels and devils with no effect is hardly the typical picture of epic warfare.

Finally, even the ultimate assault by the Son in his chariot produces a humorous image. The Son comes forth with no assistance and literally rolls over the rebels. He then herds them like "a Herd / of Goats" (856–57) down a gap toward Hell. The rebels retreat, first from the Son, then back from Hell, unwilling to confront God or place, neither here nor there. Finally, powerless to resist God, they are cast into the burning lake of Hell. The assumed power of their rebellion and fight has been nothing more than ridiculous illusion.

Throughout this battle, Milton's depiction of God's attitude has been one of easy amusement. God limits the number and power of the angel forces as if to give himself a handicap, but actually to emphasize that only his side has real power. When the rebels have small successes, God laughs. When the great geographic fight occurs, God is concerned only with the destruction of the landscape and the chaos that is being wrought. Even here, though, when God sends the Son in for the final assault, it is with limitations on the Son's power. That God will win this battle is never in doubt. That the rebels are without power against God is the lesson he teaches through the ease with which he wins the battle. The power of the rebels and the angels is controlled by God, and the rebels were both hubristic and ludicrous to think they could overthrow their creator. The battle is not treated seriously by Milton because the rebels were in no way serious opposition to God.

Theme

Metaphorically, Raphael has made his point. Satan and his cohorts rebelled, but they were no real threat to God. The real threat of the rebels was in the chaos they caused, metaphorically displayed in the uprooting of the landscape on the second day. The affront to God was in the rebellion; that is, using free will in disobedience to God produces chaos. The serious act was the disobedience to God. The battle is Raphael's way of metaphorically representing the chaos produced by disobedience, but the main point Raphael makes is that the power in the act of disobedience is illusory. At any moment he wishes, God can stop the rebellion and punish the disobedience.

The rebels are ultimately guilty of self-delusion, a self-delusion that carries over into Hell. Even though they have just been completely humiliated in battle, the fallen angels still rally to Satan in Book I. They assume that they can still challenge God's authority and oppose him by attacking Man. Their ridiculously easy defeat in battle seems forgotten by most of the rebels.

One final interesting note on Book VI is Raphael's comment that he does not name many of the angels in the battle because fame on Earth is not important when one has fame in Heaven. Conversely, he names only a few of the devils because they do not deserve fame.

Glossary

Champaign (2)   a broad plain; flat, open country.

apostate (172)   one who has abandoned his belief, faith, cause, or principles.

Cope (215)   a large, capelike vestment worn by priests at certain ceremonies; anything that covers like a cope, as a vault or the sky.

imperious (287)   overbearing, arrogant, domineering.

contemned (432)   to treat or think of with contempt; scorn.

spume (479)   to foam or froth.

vagaries (614)   an odd, eccentric, or unexpected action.

Book VII

Summary

Book VII opens with another prologue to Urania, who in classical mythology was the Muse of Astronomy but whom Milton has transformed into a heavenly or Christian inspiration. In this prologue, Milton asks Urania to bring his thoughts down from Heaven and back to Earth and to inspire him once more to rise above his physical limitations.

Returning to the scene to Eden, Adam asks Raphael to relate the story of the creation of the world. Raphael replies that after the rebellious angels were defeated, God wished to add a new creation so that no place in the universe would seem unpopulated by the absence of the fallen angels. He decided to create Mankind to live on Earth. Through obedience to God's will, Man would finally unite Earth with Heaven. God sent the Son forth to create Earth and the heavens that surround it. The Son accomplished this creation and hung Earth on a chain suspended from Heaven. Then God began the creation that would lead to Man. Raphael's account here closely follows the story of creation in *Genesis,* in which over a period of seven days, God creates the foundations of life (light, firmament, the seasons of the year, and so on) and then life itself, beginning with fish and other creatures and culminating in the creation of Man (Adam). Raphael concludes his description of the creation with an account of the rejoicing in Heaven over God's handiwork.

Commentary

The prologue to Book VII is especially interesting on two counts. First, the Muse Milton invokes is again Urania, the classical Muse of Astronomy, who is appropriate since the focus of this book is on the creation of Earth and the heavens, and Book VIII will deal with planetary motions. But, once again, just as he did in Book I, Milton disassociates Urania from the classical tradition and equates her with Christian inspiration, literally (in Book I) with the Holy Spirit. This treatment of Urania epitomizes one of Milton's goals in *Paradise Lost—*

to compose a Christian epic. He brings together the pagan classical tradition with Christian doctrine; the invocation and transmutation of Urania provides an emblematic image of this goal.

The second point of interest in this prologue is Milton's personal references. He once again alludes to his blindness with the word "darkness" in line 27, but he goes on to mention "dangers" (28) and earlier referred to "evil days." These references appear to be to the political situation in England at the time Milton wrote *Paradise Lost*. Milton had been an official in Cromwell's government and had been imprisoned briefly after the Restoration. The supporters of Charles II, as well as Charles himself, were not an especially bloodthirsty lot, but Puritans and former supporters of Cromwell had good reasons to be concerned. Milton, because of his notoriety, outspokenness, and blindness, was especially vulnerable. Moreover, his composition, a Christian epic, was not likely to be popular among the Cavaliers, who had more worldly matters on their minds. Consequently, the personal aspects of this prologue reveal Milton's sense of isolation, vulnerability, and perhaps fear at a time when, had circumstances not changed so dramatically, he might have been one of the most celebrated figures in the kingdom.

The rest of Book VII, following the prologue, needs less comment than most books since it follows the account of creation in *Genesis* quite closely. Some important differences, distinctions, and additions do exist, however. Perhaps the most apparent difference between Milton's account of creation and that in *Genesis* is that the Son, rather than God the Father, goes forth to create Earth and the heavens. Milton seems to be developing a Christian version of creation here to contrast with the Old Testament / Judaic one in *Genesis*. The Son sets forth in his chariot followed by "Cherub and Seraph, Potentates and Thrones, / And Virtues" (197–98). As he creates, the Son uses golden compasses to make Earth and the heavens surrounding it—an image that was made famous a century or so later in William Blake's illustrations for *Paradise Lost*. Following the Son's initial, triumphant creation of Earth, Milton returns to the creation account in *Genesis* in both context and cadence. As the day-by-day events are described, the actions are credited to God, although it is unclear in this section whether Milton means God the Father or God the Son.

As the events of each day of creation occur, Milton incorporates his own knowledge and interpretations. For example, in describing the creation of dry land on Day 3, Milton attributes the formation of mountains to God and also suggests that the highest mountains correspond to the lowest depths in the oceans. Neither of these ideas is in *Genesis*, and both were matters of theological debate in the seventeenth century. Milton simply adds his own ideas about geology and creation to the account. Similarly, in his account of Day 4, Milton adds scientific description and information about the stars. On Day 5, the description of certain fish is detailed and precise, reflecting Milton's study of natural history. So, on the one hand, Milton simply repeats the biblical account of creation, but, on the other, he is adding, from his own vast store of knowledge, much detailed insight and information not found in *Genesis*. In a sense, Book VII is Milton's improved scientific and Christian account of the story of creation. Of course, all of these changes are presented by Raphael, so it is more precise to call this version of creation Raphael's.

Literary Device

One last feature of Book VII, as well as of Books VI and VIII, is worth consideration. In each of these books, Adam questions Raphael concerning God, nature, and the universe. In many ways, Adam's questions seem to be simple and understandable curiosity on his part. But on a deeper level, Adam's curiosity points toward the Tree of Knowledge. Adam constantly wants more information, and this desire on his part clearly suggests that in the decisive moment, Adam's own personality may fail him. Further, Raphael, as a character, may abet Adam's eventual fall. The "affable angel" was sent by God to warn Adam of Satan's plans. Raphael has delivered and will deliver this warning piecemeal and vaguely. Raphael can explain the war in Heaven with precision. He can explain creation clearly. But he warns Adam in generalities. Raphael's vague warnings may be necessitated by God's instructions, but, even so, they lack the specificity that might truly help Adam and Eve be prepared for Satan.

Glossary

Archangel (41)   a chief angel; angel of high rank.

Hierarchies (191)   the leaders or chiefs of religious groups; high priests. Milton uses the term to represent all the angels who make up the Heavenly Host.

sapience (195)   knowledge, wisdom.

omnific (217)   creating all things.

firmament (261)   the sky, viewed poetically as a solid arch or vault.

tumid (288)   swollen; bulging.

jocund (372)   cheerful; genial.

ounce (466)   lynx or panther.

behemoth (467)   a large beast mentioned in the *Bible*; in Milton's time the term probably referred to the elephant.

hyaline (619)   transparent as glass; glassy.

Book VIII

Summary

Adam continues his conversation with Raphael in Book VIII. He asks Raphael about the movement of the stars and planets. The angel says that it doesn't matter whether Earth moves or the heavens. God has made some things unknowable. Ultimately, Raphael adds, the complexities of the universe are beyond Man's comprehension and Man should be satisfied with what God allows him to know. Then Adam tells Raphael, who was on a mission to guard Hell when God made Adam, the story of how Man was created.

Adam says that he awoke in a green and flowery bank and was immediately able to stand erect, run and jump, and, even though he was not certain who he was or where he came from, he nonetheless knew the names of the various plants and animals and could speak. Then, when he fell asleep, a dream vision appeared and led him to Eden. When Adam next woke, he saw God, who explained the creation and made the one prohibition—that Adam was not to eat from the Tree of Knowledge. Aside from that one proscription, Adam would have dominion over the rest of Earth. God then had all the animals come before Adam in pairs, and he named them, discovering that God had provided him with knowledge of the nature of each animal. At this point, Adam explained to God that he was lonely and needed a companion. God, having already planned a companion for Adam, put him to sleep. Even though unconscious, Adam was aware of what happened through the eye of his "fancy" (imagination), which God kept awake. From Adam's rib, God created a female companion, Eve, with whom Adam immediately fell in love. At first, Eve ran from Adam, but he eventually convinced her to follow him. The two experienced the feelings of love and were wedded.

Adam explains to Raphael that he is overcome with love and desire for Eve because of her physical beauty. He knows that Eve is less close to God than he, but he feels literally weakened by her attractiveness. Raphael takes issue with Adam, explaining that Eve has been created as his inferior. She is outwardly beautiful, but on the interior, spiritually, she is not Adam's equal. Raphael adds that Adam's love for Eve must rise above mere sexual desire. While once again admitting his physical attraction to Eve, Adam says that he loves her for more than the fulfillment of sexual passion. He says that his real love for Eve comes from their spiritual and intellectual companionship.

Finally, Raphael admonishes Adam to remember God's warning and to be on guard for Satan's treachery. He also tells Adam not to allow passion to overcome reason and cause him to disobey God. With that, the two beings, man and angel, part; Raphael toward Heaven, Adam to his bower.

Commentary

The astronomical discussion between Adam and Raphael reflects the scientific debate that existed in England in the seventeenth century. The discoveries and theories of Copernicus, Kepler, and Galileo were well known throughout England and Europe, but the ideas were also hotly debated. Milton, who had read extensively on the subjects and may even have met Galileo, nonetheless chooses to sidestep the issues in *Paradise Lost*. Adam and Raphael present varying viewpoints but do not reach a conclusion. Rather Raphael ends the discussion by saying that God left the questions concerning the heavens open to dispute, "perhaps to move / His laughter" (77–78). He adds that Adam should be "lowly wise" (169) and "Dream not of other worlds" (175).

Even though Milton chooses not to reach a conclusion on Adam's questions and ends the debate with homiletic advice from Raphael, it would be misleading to assume that either Milton or Raphael intends to discourage questions about the universe. Milton's interest in science is well established, and Raphael seems pleased with the questions that Adam asks. It was commonplace in the Restoration period to refer to nature as God's Book of Works, which was entirely compatible with God's Book of Words (the Bible). So questions about nature and the heavens were not considered presumptuous, though they could lead to incorrect, even evil, conclusions. Therefore, Adam, in opening up the abstruse topic of the geocentric / heliocentric universe is advised to stick to more down-to-earth queries—not to avoid questions at all.

By today's standards, Raphael's (God's) advice to Adam seems to limit Man's ability to learn, but, within the context of the time, God suggests that Man should be content with what he *can* learn about the world rather than what must remain theory. In other words, Man should learn the practical ways of the physical world and leave metaphysical concerns to God.

The idea that God laughs at Man's attempts to theorize about the universe continues Milton's problematic portrayal of God the Father. How to make an omniscient being who is the embodiment of pure reason empathetic is a difficult task. God the Father often seems austere and condescending although those qualities are built into the notion of making the Supreme Being a fictional character. God the Son, who will become Man, naturally seems more human, and perhaps the Son is Milton's way of humanizing the Father.

Character Insight

Eve's attitude toward the conversation between Adam and Raphael is frequently misunderstood. She walks away as the discussion of planetary motion begins, and some readers have assumed that the subject is beyond her female understanding. However, Milton says directly that such is not the case. Rather, Eve prefers to hear the explanation privately and directly from Adam. This explanation is consistent with Milton's attitude toward Eve and women in general throughout the work. Women are intellectually inferior to men but not significantly. Eve is interested in the subject, but will both enjoy the explanation more and understand it better if Adam explains it to her. This attitude also establishes the role of Eve and women as helpmates to their husbands. The husband's role is in the world; the wife's at home. But, within the privacy of the home, the two may operate on equal footing as the anticipated conversation between Adam and Eve would prove.

Adam's description of his creation is similar to Raphael's description of the creation of Earth in Book VII—both accounts follow the biblical versions but also contain significant additions by Milton. Milton shows Adam standing erect, running, jumping, discovering his reason, and deducing information about the world into which he has just been created. Further, Milton adds Adam's trance-like sleep and the Divine Guide who takes Adam to Eden and explains creation to him.

The scene in which Adam asks God for a companion is one of the intentionally lighthearted scenes in *Paradise Lost*. In this scene, God is like a teacher or parent who already knows the answer to a child's request but wants to make the child work a bit before revealing it. God knows that Adam needs companionship but makes him go through a scholarly disputation to explain the reasoning behind his need. Adam argues well and pleases God through the use of his reason.

Some commentators on *Paradise Lost* have been troubled by Adam's statement at line 415. In explaining why God does not need companionship, Adam says, "Thou in Thyself art perfect." To some, this line suggest Unitarianism, especially when coupled with Adam's further comment to God that God is, "through all numbers absolute, though one" (421). In examining the context, however, it seems doubtful that Milton actually intended to challenge the doctrine of the Trinity here. Rather, Adam is establishing the basic difference between Man and God. God is perfect and, by definition, needs nothing else to be complete; Man is imperfect and needs companionship and much more. Many critics have pointed out that Milton is following Aristotle's discussion of God in the *Eudemian Ethics* and probably did not consider the lines' implications in terms of the Trinity.

Character Insight

For Adam, Eve is the greatest of God's creations on Earth. As Adam explains his love for Eve to Raphael, both the angel and the reader become aware of how Adam's feelings for Eve pose a danger for him. Adam adores Eve. His paean to her character and beauty reaches the level of adulation. Adam does note some of the ways that Eve is inferior to him, but the overall tenor of his description reveals a depth of love that makes Raphael frown with concern. Milton uses Adam's feelings for Eve to set up the temptation scene in Book IX. To this point, Adam has been presented as a strong and intelligent character, able to debate successfully with God. Adam has listened and learned from Raphael. Further, he has heard and understood Raphael's warnings. Adam knows that he and Eve must not be disobedient to God's command. The question, thus, is how, given the strength of Adam's character, how can he believably yield to temptation in Book IX?

Character Insight

The answer to this question lies mainly in Adam's discussion of Eve in Book VIII. The reader knows from Book I that Eve is vain and moreover that she is in a number of ways inferior to Adam. She needs Adam's help and counsel so the idea that she might be deluded by Satan is not farfetched. Adam's weakness is not so obvious until Book VIII when he tells Raphael about Eve. If *Paradise Lost* were a Greek tragedy, Adam's love for Eve would be his flaw. His reason can be overcome by Eve's beauty. His sexual passion for her literally makes him weak. Through this passion, Milton makes the point that love, especially love expressed as sexual desire, can be excessive. Raphael tells Adam that his love for Eve's beauty may be excessive, and Adam tries to explain that his spiritual and intellectual love for her is even greater. However,

Adam's attempt to put his love for Eve on a higher plane seems an after-thought. The focus of Adam's speech on Eve makes Raphael and the reader fully aware that Adam's reason can be swayed by his excessive passion for Eve.

For modern readers, Raphael's warning to Adam about sexual passion may seem old fashioned, even prudish, but the reality of the problem—that a man can lose his reason over a woman (and vice versa)—is only as far away as today's newspaper. Milton's point that love, especially the love that is driven by sexual desire, can cause people to act without reason is an idea both ancient and modern. Raphael again warns Adam of danger from Satan, and Adam promises vigilance, but Milton has carefully set the stage for the drama that will take place in Book IX.

As Raphael prepares to leave, Adam asks about love and sex among the angels, and Raphael blushes, "rosy red" (620). This brief, suggestive interlude is like comic relief in a tragedy, a last, lighthearted moment before the serious matters of Book IX.

Glossary

corporeal (109)   physical; bodily; not spiritual.

obliquities (132)   not level or upright; inclined.

transpicuous (141)   transparent; esp., easily understood.

fealty (344)   loyalty; fidelity.

solace (419)   an easing of grief, loneliness, discomfort.

colloquy (455)   a conversation, esp. a formal discussion.

abash't (595)   embarrassed and ill at ease; abashed.

Hesperian (632)   may refer to the Cape Verde Islands which were called the Hesperides; or could, in context, simply mean the setting sun, which is the older meaning of the word.

Book IX

Summary

In the prologue to Book IX, Milton says that his work must now take a tragic tone and that this Christian epic, though different, is nonetheless more heroic than earlier epics like the *Iliad* and the *Aeneid*. Again, he calls on Urania as the muse of Christian inspiration to help him complete his work and show the true heroism that lies in the Christian idea of sacrifice. Then Milton returns to his story.

Satan returns to Eden eight days after being forced out by Gabriel. He has studied all the animals and has decided to approach Eve in the form of a serpent which he considers to be the "subtlest Beast of all the Field" (86).

The following morning, Adam and Eve prepare for their daily work tending the Garden. Because the Garden's growth seems to surpass their labors, Eve suggests that on this day they work apart. She thinks they can accomplish more working individually. Adam argues the point with Eve, saying that Raphael has warned them of dangers and that she is more vulnerable by herself. He and she continue this argument—she proposing that they work alone; he proposing that they work together—until Adam finally relents; however, he makes Eve promise to return to their bower soon, but Milton comments that she will never return to Adam in the way that she was that morning.

Satan in the form of the serpent is surprised and excited to find Eve alone tending flowers. He watches her and for a few moments becomes enraptured and forgets his evil nature. Then he remembers what his purpose is—to destroy God's creation. The serpent approaches Eve upright upon its tail. His various acts fail to attract Eve's attention because she is used to dealing with animals. However, when the serpent speaks, complimenting Eve on her beauty, playing on both her vanity and curiosity, Eve is suddenly interested. She is especially curious about how the serpent learned to speak. Satan replies through the serpent that he learned speech by eating the fruit of a particular tree in the Garden. He acquired speech and the ability to reason and has, therefore, sought Eve out to worship as the most beautiful of God's creations.

When Eve inquires which tree gave the serpent his abilities, he takes her to the Tree of Knowledge. Eve tells the serpent that God has forbidden Man to eat from that tree, and she chooses to obey God. Satan, using the same sophistic reasoning he has used throughout the story, tells Eve that God has tricked her and Adam. He has eaten of the tree and is not dead; neither will they die. Instead the tree will give them knowledge, which will make them like God. This fact makes God envious and has caused him to demand that Adam and Eve not eat of the tree. Eve is taken in by the words of the serpent, and after some rationalizing, she convinces herself that she should eat the fruit. And she does.

Now Eve suddenly worships the Tree of Knowledge as a god, even as all nature weeps for her fall. Her thoughts turn to Adam, and she decides that he must eat the fruit also. She cannot bear the idea that she might die and Adam would be given another wife. When Eve approaches Adam, he drops the wreath of flowers that he was weaving for her hair. Eve quickly tells him what she has done, and Adam just as quickly makes his own decision. He allows his physical love and passion for Eve to outweigh his reason. He knowingly eats the fruit and is immediately affected with carnal desire for Eve. The two humans exit to engage in "amorous play" (1045). The description here is not of love but lust.

After sex, Adam and Eve fall into a deep sleep. They awake and are overcome with shame and guilty knowledge. They both are weeping, and they launch into arguments with each other. Adam says Eve is at fault; she replies in kind. Milton describes them as spending "fruitless hours" (1188) in bitter accusation. Each is willing to blame the other, but neither is willing to accept responsibility. Paradise is gone and in its place guilt, blame, and shame. Milton says that both of them have given way to "Appetite" (1129), and reason is lost. Paradise has ended; the earth has begun.

Commentary

Milton's fourth invocation differs from earlier ones in that he does not call on Urania, except obliquely, and he does not mention his blindness. Rather he offers an explanation for his epic and says that the tone must now become "Tragic" (6). The word "tragic" had two connotations for Milton. First, it carried the simple moral meaning of something terribly bad or unfortunate. Christians since the Middle Ages had always considered the falls of Lucifer and Adam tragic. But "tragic" also refers to the dramatic concept of tragedy as first defined by Aristotle and developed through the centuries to its high achievement in Elizabethan England. Milton knew the nature of dramatic tragedy from his study of the Greeks (he patterned *Samson Agonistes* on Greek tragedy) as well as from reading Shakespeare and other Elizabethan dramatists (he wrote an essay *On Shakespeare* for the Second Folio).

By the seventeenth century, tragedies had assumed a basic format. The play would have a noble hero who had a tragic flaw in either personality or actions. The fortunes of the hero would reverse during the play from good to bad with the hero recognizing his own responsibility for these consequences that resulted from his flaw. The end of the play would result in the death of the hero. Throughout the play, fate would, in one form or another, control the action, and, at the end, the audience would experience a *catharsis* or purging of emotions, resulting from their empathy with the hero. They should feel pity for the hero and fear for themselves.

To see that *Paradise Lost* has an underlying tragic structure is not difficult. Adam is a noble character. He has a flaw in his passion for Eve that overrides his reason. He makes the mistake of eating the fruit. He recognizes, eventually, his responsibility for his actions. Death, though not occurring in the epic, is the main result of Adam's action. Fate (God) knows what will happen throughout the poem. And finally, Milton wanted his audience to experience pity for Adam and all mankind but fear for the consequences of their own sinful lives. So when Milton speaks of changing his "Notes to Tragic" (6), he means more than a passing remark.

Yet for all of these connections to tragedy, *Paradise Lost* is not a tragedy; it is a Christian epic with a tragic core. Adam is a noble hero, but as Milton notes in this prologue, he is not a hero like Achilles, Aeneas, or Odysseus. He is, in Milton's words, a hero of "Patience and Heroic Martyrdom" (33). Ultimately too, Adam is regenerated and reconciled rather than just killed. *Paradise Lost* will end on a hopeful—even joyful—note, since through Adam's fall, salvation and eternal life will come to Man through God's mercy and grace. This *felix culpa* or "happy fault" is not the stuff of tragedy.

Moreover, even as an epic, Milton says that he was attempting something different in *Paradise Lost*. He did not want to glorify warfare as in earlier epics like the *Iliad*. Instead, in his only description of warfare (Book VI), he creates parody rather than magnificence. Rather Milton's goal was to write a Christian epic, specifically a *Protestant* Christian epic with a new sort of hero, one who wins ultimately through patience and suffering. At the time Milton wrote this particular invocation, he still prayed to the Muse (Urania, Christian inspiration) to help him complete his work and to let it gain acceptance in a time when such a work's fate was unclear.

After the invocation, Milton begins this book with Satan who has been absent for the three books in which Adam and Raphael talked. Satan has degenerated as a character. In his speech in Eden, he is unable to make his thoughts logical. He thinks Earth may be more beautiful than Heaven since God created it after Heaven. He thinks he might be happy on Earth but then argues that he could not be happy in Heaven. He fusses about Man being tended by angels. Satan's ability to think, which seemed potent in Book I, now appears weak and confused. An even greater indication of Satan's character degeneration is that he is now self-delusional. In the early books, he lied but only to get others to do his bidding. In this speech, he lies to himself. He questions whether God actually created the angels, he sees Man as God's revenge on him, he says he took half of all the angels out of Heaven. Satan who seemed somewhat heroic in his rebellion now seems to be a dangerous con man who has come to believe his own lies. In the early books, the reader can at least see reasoning as well as envy behind Satan's actions, but, here in Book IX, Satan has become the delusional psychopath who believes his own lies. The concept of heroism cannot be stretched to include Satan's attitude and thinking at this point in the epic.

Milton reinforces Satan's degeneration with visual images. Satan creeps along the ground of Eden in a low-lying mist and ultimately takes on the form of the serpent who crawls along the ground. The shape changes Satan has made in *Paradise Lost* show a pattern. From angel to cherub, from cherub to cormorant, then to lion and tiger, and finally to toad and snake, Satan has progressively made himself more and more earthbound and lowly. The irony of these shifts in shape is not lost on Satan. As he searches for a serpent to enter, he complains of the bestial nature of the animal that he must "incarnate and imbrute, / That to the highth of deity aspired" (166–167). That is, as he tries to become like God, he takes on lower and lower forms.

Character Insight

The next scene of Book IX involves the argument between Adam and Eve over whether they should work alone or separately. Some commentators have seen Eve's arguments as a kind of calculated sophistry akin to Satan's that demonstrates Eve's complicity in her own fall. Her argument, however, is more of innocence. She has played the proper womanly role during Raphael's visit, and now she simply wants more freedom and responsibility. Perhaps she wants to show that she can be Adam's equal. To read Eve as a conniver is to overlook her naiveté and innocent desire to be more like Adam.

Satan's attitude when he finds Eve alone shows that the two humans made the wrong decision in separating. When Satan sees Eve by herself, he is pleased that she is not with Adam, who would have been a "Foe not informidable" (486). Eve's only real defense against Satan seems to be her basic beauty and goodness. Satan is so astounded when he first sees her that for a brief period he forgets his purpose and stands "Stupidly good" (465). The scene makes two points: First, the goodness expressed just by Eve's physical person is overwhelming. And second, Satan has lost the capacity for real goodness. He may be momentarily struck dumb and be "stupidly good," but he quickly recovers and is not in any way deflected from his evil purpose.

Literary Device

Satan's temptation of Eve is a cunning masterpiece. As a prelapsarian serpent, he is able to approach her standing upright upon his tail, a "Circular base of rising folds, that tow'r'd / Fold above fold, a surging maze" (498–99). The images of circuitous, folding mazes occur intermittently throughout *Paradise Lost* and reach their culmination in this image of the serpent rising to tempt Eve with his body a coiling labyrinth. Visually, Eve is pure, simple innocence; the serpent, unfathomable, complex evil. Eve will soon be lost in his labyrinthine argument and plot.

Satan as serpent first uses his physical beauty and speech to impress Eve, who finds him beautiful. A number of writers have found sexual undertones in the description of the serpent: "pleasing was his shape, / And lovely" (503–04). An old Jewish tradition even had it that Eve made love with the serpent. Milton's subtle sexualizing of the serpent followed this tradition and adds another element to Eve's fall. William Blake, in his illustration for this scene, certainly noticed sexual imagery. At first glance, Eve appears to kiss the serpent, but is, in fact, taking a bite of a very phallic apple in the serpent's mouth. The fruit hanging from the Tree of Life in Blake's illustration suggests nothing so much as male genitalia.

Eve is also taken with the fact that the serpent talks. Further, the snake is not in the angelic form of the tempter in Eve's dream, so she is not put on guard by the creature. (Milton has made it clear earlier that Adam and Eve were never threatened by any animal in Eden.) Satan first flatters Eve. He licks the ground. He says he worships her beauty. The reader recalls that Eve narcissistically became enamored of her own image in the water at her creation. She is vain, but she is also second-ary to Adam. Here a talking snake praises her beauty and says he wor-ships her. She is interested though not enraptured.

But when the serpent takes Eve to the Tree of Knowledge, his argu-ments come so fast and so deviously that she cannot follow them. At first, she does what she should. She tells the serpent that she cannot eat from the tree. He argues that he has eaten and did not die. Then he adds that God wants her to eat of the tree and, contradictorily, that he envies what the humans might learn if they did eat. The arguments come so fast that Eve cannot answer, let alone think through them. Her innocence in comparison with Satan's cunning overcomes her reason. She is no match for Satan, and so his sophistic arguments seem reason to her. Unlike Adam, Eve buys into the arguments without grasping what is really happening. Eve eats the fruit, and eats, for the first time, gluttonously, letting her appetite take control of her reason.

After she eats, Eve at first feels elated. She thinks that she has reached a higher level but shows this ironically by starting to worship the tree. Her thoughts turn to Adam. Initially, she thinks she might keep this new power for herself and perhaps become his equal. At this point, Eve is conniving; already the fruit has changed her innocence. Even her rea-son for telling Adam shows this fact. If the fruit indeed leads to death, she does not want to die and leave Adam to another woman. She self-ishly wants him to be in the same condition she is.

Adam's temptation and fall is much less complicated than Eve's. When Adam drops the flowery chaplet that he has been making for Eve, he symbolically drops all that he has in Eden. He immediately real-izes what Eve has done. Adam makes a conscious decision to eat the fruit because he cannot give up Eve. He allows his physical passion for her to outweigh his reason, and so he eats. Adam's decision is willful, unlike Eve's, which was based on fraudulent argument and weak reason.

After the fall, the two are overcome by lust. Adam says to Eve, "if such pleasure be / In things to us forbidden, it might be wish'd, / For this one Tree had been forbidden ten" (1024–26). The language of the entire scene is charged with sexual imagery and innuendo. Their appetites are in control, and reason is lost. After their lovemaking, they fall into a troubled sleep—no more innocent dreams. When they wake, they are cognizant of what they have done, and their arguing is that of real people. If their argument at the end of Book IX is compared with their discussion of whether to work alone or together at the beginning, the difference in Man before and after the fall is clear. The opening discussion is reasoned and pleasant; the closing, irrational and bitter.

Glossary

harbinger (13)   a person or thing that comes before to announce or give an indication of what follows; herald.

sedulous (27)   working hard and steadily; diligent.

Seneschal (38)   a steward or major-domo in the household of a medieval noble.

wanton (211)   [Now Rare] luxuriant (said of vegetation, etc.).

patriarch (376)   the father and ruler of a family or tribe; Adam is identified in *Paradise Lost* as the *patriarch* of all Mankind.

verdant (500)   covered with green vegetation.

unctuous (635)   oily or greasy; made up of or containing fat or oil. Milton uses the word to describe one of the elements of *ignis fatuus* or *fool's fire*, a phenomenon like St. Elmo's Fire which often led the foolish astray.

dalliance (1016)   flirting, toying, or trifling. Milton uses the term as a euphemism for sex.

umbrage (1087)   shade; shadow; foliage, considered as shade-giving.

Book X

Summary

The first scene of Book X takes place in Heaven, where the angels are aware of Adam's and Eve's fall. God assembles the hosts to confirm this fact and to emphasize that he knew Adam and Eve would yield to temptation but that he in no way inclined them to the deed. The act was of their own free wills. Now, however, Adam and Eve must be judged; however, God adds, justice can be tempered with mercy. God sends the Son to pronounce sentence on Adam and Eve.

The Son quickly descends to Eden where he pronounces judgment. God (the Son) first condemns the serpent who allowed Satan to use his body. The snake will now crawl on its belly rather than go upright. Further God establishes an eternal enmity between women (represented by Eve) and serpents. Eve's children will bruise the serpent's head; the serpent, their heel. Eve and all women will be given the pain of childbirth as well as subjugation to their husbands. Finally, men, because of Adam, will have to labor in the ground to make their food and be subject to death, literally returning to the dust from which they were created. As a final act, done so kindly that it presages God's ultimate mercy, the Son clothes Adam and Eve in animal skins.

The scene now switches from Earth to Hell, where Sin and Death, having finished the causeway between Hell and Earth, start toward Earth. En route, they see Satan in his angelic form, winging toward Hell. Satan reveals the events that have transpired, and Sin congratulates her father on his accomplishments and suggests, falsely, that his power has allowed her and Death to escape Hell. She adds, also falsely, that Satan now controls all of humanity while God controls Heaven. Satan is pleased with Sin's comments and tells her to hurry to Earth with Death so that they can take control. He meanwhile proceeds on into Hell.

As Satan enters Hell, it appears deserted, and he has to go all the way into Pandemonium to find the other fallen angels. As the fallen angels see Satan, they welcome him joyously, and he addresses them with a gloating speech filled with pride. He tells them of the temptation of Eve and how he caused both humans to fall with a lowly apple.

He says that the rebellious angels can now occupy Paradise (Eden). Expecting applause and plaudits of the assembled demons, Satan hears hissing instead. Snakes are crawling all through Pandemonium, and Satan and his followers are quickly turned into snakes. Trees like the Tree of Knowledge sprout up, but when the snakes eat the tempting fruit, it turns to bitter soot and ash. This scene essentially ends the role of Satan and the fallen angels in the narrative.

Meanwhile, Sin and Death have reached Earth where they see a fertile field for their exploits. God sees the children of Satan on Earth and tells the angels that, because of the fall of Adam and Eve, Sin and Death will continue to live on Earth until the Judgment Day, when they will be cast into Hell with their father and sealed up, never to exit. With this prophecy from God, Sin and Death are seen no more in the poem.

God then tells the angels to transform the Earth. They are to create the seasons and different types of violent weather. Discord is also brought to Earth so that animals will now hunt and kill each other and menace Man. Adam is aware of all these changes and blames himself. He begins with lamentation for what he has done and the consequences. He wishes to take all the blame for what has happened on himself; then he thinks of Eve and feels that she was wicked and deserves blame also. Adam finds himself in a hopeless state. When Eve tries to speak to him, he rebuffs her angrily and questions why God created females.

Eve approaches Adam again and makes what is known as the "Regeneration Speech." She begs Adam not to turn away from her. She explains that the serpent tricked her. She begs Adam to stay with her, that even in their pain they can love each other. She says that she would take all the punishment on herself because she sinned against God and Adam while Adam sinned only against God. Adam is moved by Eve's words, and his feelings for her return. He tells her that they must stop blaming each other. They can become a comfort one to the other and, through love, lighten the burden of death that has been put on them.

When Eve suggests that they might avoid God's curse on the world by either remaining childless or by committing suicide, Adam responds by saying that they should not try to cheat God. He reminds Eve that God said her offspring would bruise the head of the serpent. He analyzes that by the serpent, God meant Satan. Therefore, if they live and produce offspring, eventually their children will bruise the head of the serpent and Satan will be defeated. He then concludes that they should pray and seek God's grace and mercy, which they do.

Commentary

In several ways, Book X is the culmination of the plot of *Paradise Lost*, with Books XI and XII being an extended denouement or resolution. Milton constructs Book X as a series of short culminating scenes that provide the final appearances for a number of major characters. After Book X, Satan, Sin, Death, the rebellious angels, and, for the most part, God and the Son, will be gone from the story.

Style & Language

The technique Milton uses in Book X contrasts with the stagy-dramatic nature of Book IX, which contained many long soliloquies or monologues by various characters. Book X contains more brief scenes with fewer speeches. The nature of epic writing allows for these shifts in style, focus, and point of view. Because the epic is conceived on such a grand scale, many different styles and even genres can be incorporated within the single work. Book IX contains all the elements of a tragedy, but *Paradise Lost* is not tragedy. A tragedy would end with the fall of Adam and Eve and the arrival of Death in the world, not with the regeneration of the two humans and a promise of ultimate triumph. An epic can contain a tragedy within its structure but still be much more than just a tragedy. Likewise, an epic can contain sections of long set speeches linked to other sections where the action moves with movie-like speed. The epic structure puts demands on both reader and writer, but it also allows for more variety for both as well.

The first three scenes of Book X provide interesting contrasts. In the first scene, God sends the Son to judge Adam, Eve, and the serpent. This judgment takes place in the second scene. In the third scene, Sin and Death meet Satan returning to Hell. These second and third scenes seem intended to be complementary. In both, a creator / father meets with two of his creations / children. In both scenes, the creator provides judgment, advice, and information about the future to the children.

The Son, who in Book VII is revealed as the creator of Earth and of Adam and Eve, is sent forth by the Father to pronounce judgment upon the humans and the serpent. The serpent is judged because he allowed another being to take control of his nature. The reasoning here is quite similar to that behind many of the punishments Dante describes in the eighth circle of Hell in the *Inferno*. For Dante, and for Milton as well, fraud is involved in allowing one's nature to be usurped, even if that usurpation is unwitting, as the serpent's seems to be.

The Son passes judgment on his own creation (Adam and Eve) as kindly as possible. He is not vengeful, but more fatherly in explaining what the punishment is and why it must occur. After passing judgment, the Son clothes the couple, an act comparable to Jesus washing the feet of the disciples. Besides the literal clothing of Adam and Eve, the Son also clothes their inward nakedness with a "Robe of Righteousness" which will protect them from God's wrath. The Son here acts "[a]s Father of his Family" (216), and this act begins to show Adam and Eve that grace and mercy are still open to them.

Literary Device

In the following scene, another father meets his children. Satan finds Sin and Death constructing their bridge to Earth. The interrelationship between parent and children here is in direct contrast with the previous scene. The symbolism of the bridge that Sin and Death construct is straightforward. Once Sin and Death enter Earth, the pathway to Hell will be broad and easily traveled, accommodating the millions who will use it. The children of Satan are excited by the prospects of what their father has accomplished, even though both Sin and Satan lie to each other. Sin praises Satan for his "magnific deeds" (354) on Earth. She also tells him that he empowered them to build the bridge and that now Satan rules Earth while God rules Heaven. All that Sin tells her father are lies to build his ego. Her speech is an unwitting set up, raising his self-delusions to their highest pitch just before he will be brought low. The blatant exaggeration and lying here contrasts sharply with the somber, reasoned, and hopeful speech of the Son to Adam and Eve. Further, Satan sends his two children forth to rule Earth, through destruction, promising them that they will "Reign in bliss" (399), an exaggerated lie on his part as the reader will learn in a few more lines. The contrast is between truth with the Son, Adam, and Eve; lies with Satan, Sin, and Death.

Satan's entrance into Hell is not triumphant; the other rebellious angels have retreated into Pandemonium. Satan shifts to the lowest form of angel to walk among his followers and is not recognized. Then, at the moment he reveals himself on his throne and makes his boasting, gloating speech, his last shape change occurs, but this time he does not cause it. Rather God turns Satan into the serpent form he had occupied in Eden. Along with Satan all the rebels are made snakes, too. Satan had misunderstood God's judgment on the serpent; it was also judgment on Satan. Now he and his followers will go along the ground. The heel of Woman will bruise his head, and though Satan does not realize it, the woman who will bruise his head will be Mary, the Second Eve and mother of Jesus. The glorious plan to become like God has resulted in the rebellious angels having the form of the most detested of earthbound creatures, the reviled snake. And rather than ruling in glory, they will be destroyed by Man as part of the Son's judgment. In his moment of personal triumph, Satan is brought low by God.

Style & Language

Milton creates the scene of the demons turned into snakes with a particularly effective use of sibilance, the alliterative repetition of "s" sounds. Beginning with line 508, "A dismal, universal hiss, the sound / Of public scorn" (508–509) and continuing through line 520, "transformed / Alike to Serpents, all as accessories," Milton repeats the sound of "s" with such persistence that, if the passage is read out loud, the reader literally hisses along with the snakes. It is an especially effective and purposeful use of alliteration.

This scene ends with a forest filled with Trees of Knowledge appearing before the snakes, the fruit of which turns to bitter ash when the snakes try to eat it. The bitter ash represents the result of all the evil that Satan has done. He is not the ruler of Earth; he and his followers are still controlled by God. This scene is the last appearance of Satan and the rebels in *Paradise Lost*. They end their role in the epic totally defeated by the power of God. Even though they will be allowed to regain their forms, the book suggests that they will be forced into the shape of serpents at regular intervals. Further, their only reward, besides lack of control of their bodies, is the bitter ash from the tree.

The next scene is the final one for Sin and Death. Their gloating on Earth is listened to by God who pronounces their ultimate fate, to be sealed up in Hell on Judgment Day. The sense here is that Milton is working his way through the loose ends and characters of the plot so he can concentrate on Adam and the future of Mankind in the last two books.

The next scene deals with Earth. Earth was created as a perfect place for God's perfect creation. It too has to be transformed. So God sends angels to bring about the necessary transformations: seasons, bad weather, a tilted axis. Here Milton demonstrates again his scientific knowledge and explains much of the natural phenomena and problems on Earth as part of the judgment that occurred when Man fell.

Last Milton returns to Adam and Eve. This scene does not end the story of the two humans. Their story continues through the last two books. But here, in Book X, Milton shows the reconciliation that must occur between Adam and Eve if God's ultimate plan is to work. That is, if Man is to bruise the head of the serpent, Adam and Eve have to produce offspring to populate the Earth. They cannot remain alienated and in despair.

Interestingly, Milton chooses Eve as the agent of reconciliation. Adam's monologue of despair shows that his reason is broken and despair has set in. Eve embodies not reason but love. Her love that shines through as she begs Adam to forgive her helps regenerate Adam. Through Eve's love, Adam begins to find hope. As Adam accepts what Eve offers, his ability to reason returns. Eve, who sinned against Adam and God, has now redeemed herself with Adam. Once again, she stands in proper relationship to her husband. Here she makes the argument for suicide, but Adam, once again utilizing reason and wisdom, explains why suicide is not right. If God's plan to destroy Satan, Sin, and Death is to be realized, it will occur through Man. They have an obligation to accept their punishment, populate the earth, and begin the process that will redeem themselves and all Mankind. Their prayer at the end of Book X begins their reconciliation with God.

Glossary

intercessor (96)   one who pleads or makes a request in behalf of another or others.

discount'nanc't (110)   ashamed or embarrassed; disconcerted.

oracle (182)   any person or agency believed to be in communication with a deity.

sagacious (281)   having or showing keen perception or discernment and sound judgment.

Causey (415)   a causeway.

plebeian (442)   one of the common people.

efficacy (660)   effectiveness.

Synod (661)   any assembly or council. Milton uses the word to describe a meeting or conjunction of the stars astrologically.

redound (739)   to come back; react; recoil (upon).

Book XI

Summary

Adam and Eve offer fervent, sincere prayers to God for forgiveness. In Heaven, God hears the prayers. The Son intercedes with the Father to show grace and mercy to the humans, saying that he will make up for any inadequacies in Man through his own incarnation and death. God accepts the Son's intercession but says that Adam and Eve cannot remain in Eden. They must still suffer the judgments God has proclaimed, and they must die. However, if they lead a good life, they will be able to live with God for eternity. God summons all the angels to hear his final pronouncement and assigns Michael to go to Earth and expel Adam and Eve from the Garden.

After their prayers, Adam and Eve are more reconciled with their new situation. Adam encourages Eve, reminding her that she will be the mother of Mankind and that her offspring will bruise the serpent. Eve answers that she does not feel worthy to be so honored because she has brought Sin and Death into the world. Eve adds that she will be content to live out her allotted life in Eden.

Michael arrives at this point and informs Adam and Eve of God's decree that they must leave Eden. Eve is stunned, lamenting the loss of the flowers, her bridal bower, everything she holds dear. Adam is also shocked but understands that God's decree must be obeyed. He thanks Michael for informing them so gently and adds that he worries that, outside of Eden, he will never be able to talk with or see God again. Michael assures Adam that God is everywhere on Earth. The angel then puts Eve into a peaceful sleep and takes Adam to the highest point in Paradise from which Michael will give Adam a vision of the future of Mankind.

The first part of Adam's vision is of Cain and Abel. Adam sees Cain's murder of Abel and then is told by Michael that the killer and victim are Adam's own sons. Adam laments the brutality of what he has seen and is then given a further vision of all the terrible ways in which death will take humans. Adam is in deep sorrow over what he has caused and asks if there is no other way for a man to die. Michael responds that those who live good and temperate lives may drop "like ripe fruit" (535). Adam answers that he will neither seek death nor fear life but live in the best manner he can, an idea to which the angel assents.

Next, Adam is shown a vision based on Genesis IV, 20–22, an account of the children of Cain who discovered metalwork. The vision shows men on a plain working with metals and playing musical instruments. Then from the hills that border the plain come a group of Godly men. Beautiful women emerge from tents on the plain, and soon the men pair off and go with the women into the tents. Adam finds this scene much more pleasant than the first. Michael admonishes Adam not to be taken in by a life of pleasure. The people in the vision learned a useful skill but then allowed their craft to become an art, which was more important to them than God. They were the children of Cain.

The men who came down from the hills were the children of Adam and Eve's third child, Seth. They were God-fearing men. Michael calls the women, also descendants of Cain, "Atheists" (625) who have been trained in the arts of sexual love. They lure the men from their godly lives. Adam understands Michael's point, saying that man's downfall starts with women. Michael develops this idea by referring to the fallen men's "effeminate slackness" (634), through which men give over their superiority to women and thus yield to sin. The deeper point, concerning sexual desire, that applies to the story of Adam and Eve is not lost on Adam.

Michael now shows Adam a scene of violence—a terrible battle followed by futile negotiations. Only one man speaks with reason. He is Enoch, whose speech for reconciliation is met with such vehement opposition that he faces death until God takes him to Heaven in a cloud. The story of Enoch shifts directly into the story of Noah. By Noah's time, the Earth is filled with decadence and depravity. Only Noah speaks out against the evil that is taking place. God is so revolted by the actions of Mankind that he sends a flood to destroy everyone but Noah and his family. Adam sees the flood and cries out in anguish at the evil that occurs because of his and Eve's fall. All of his children fall into sin and are destroyed, and he has to watch with no way to help.

Michael says that while all of the evil have perished, nonetheless, the righteous man, Noah, survived because he remained obedient to God. Michael goes through the entire story of Noah. The story ends with an account of the rainbow, God's covenant with Noah, and through him all humans, not to destroy the Earth with flood or fire again until all sin is destroyed by the fire at the end of time. Adam is somewhat comforted by the story of Noah's survival. He is pleased that the just have been saved and the world continues.

Commentary

Books XI and XII change the focus of *Paradise Lost*. The plot of Adam's and Eve's fall has been completed. The final scenes for most characters have occurred. A brief conclusion seems logical. Instead, Milton adds two more books that trace biblical history through Jesus. Many scholars and readers have questioned the artistic justification for these books, and, in truth, the books do seem to needlessly prolong the work. On the other hand, several solid arguments can be adduced to explain the reasons for Books XI and XII, if not their necessity.

Milton's stated purpose in the poem is to justify God's ways to Man. By the end of Book X, Milton has been able to explain his concept of what God did and why, but he has offered little in the way of justification. Can the single instance of disobedience by Eve and then Adam justify death, war, plague, famine—an endless list of evil? To truly accomplish his goal, Milton needs to show the effects of the fall on Adam and Eve over a longer period and at the same time develop the notion that some greater good than innocence and immortality in Paradise could result from the fall. Books XI and XII represent Milton's attempt at justification.

The justification of God's ways is developed in two ways. First, the justification of God's acts is presented to Adam as a part of the plot structure. That is, through the visions Michael shows Adam, Adam gains a greater individual understanding of what he did, why it was wrong, what the consequences are for him and for all Mankind, and why those consequences are truly better than what would have happened if Adam and Eve had remained sinless in the Garden. Second, the justification for God's ways is developed in a broader scope for the reader as a representative for all Mankind. Through Adam's actions and consequences, the reader gets Milton's explanation of why Man fell and why sin, death, and the myriad of other evils exist on Earth. Through Adam's vision, the reader also sees how Adam's sin will be repeated in various ways and various times throughout history. It is in these final two books that Milton completes his argument for his audience and either does or does not achieve the justification he set as his goal.

Character Insight

In Book XI, Michael is introduced as the second angel, after Raphael, to impart information and education to Adam. Michael and Raphael make an interesting contrast. Both come with messages for Adam, and both speak to Adam outside of Eve's presence. Michael is stern though not unkind while Raphael is often called the "affable archangel." Michael brings pronouncements to Adam; Raphael engaged Adam in a friendly conversation. Michael's statements to Adam are straightforward lessons that cannot be misconstrued; Raphael is much less authoritarian in his tone, causing a number of critics to partially blame Raphael for Adam's failure to be prepared for the serpent. Michael cannot be faulted for lack of clarity. The contrast points up the differences in Man's relationship with the angels before and after the fall. Before the fall, Man had a more personal relationship with Heaven; after the fall, Heaven instructs, Man listens.

Theme

The absence of Eve when both Raphael and Michael talk with Adam reinforces the idea that woman is secondary to man. During Raphael's visit, Eve absents herself, preferring to have Raphael's ideas explained to her by Adam. Michael puts Eve into a deep sleep while he talks with Adam. Once again the idea is that Eve will better understand if the message is provided for her by Adam. In Milton's view of biblical and world history, women have an important role, but in matters of the intellect, men predominate.

A further aspect of Milton's view of women's role in society comes in the second vision that Michael presents. In this vision, a group of godly men are seduced by a group of seductive women. Adam's positive response to this scene points up his weakness for women that led to his fall. Michael says that men often will fall away from God by yielding their superior position to women because of physical and sexual attraction. Michael calls this "effeminate slackness" (634) in men and suggests that the problem results from the reversal of the proper or ordained order of the world. Among humans, men have a certain superiority over women. Milton's ideas on the roles of men and women have provoked much critical debate through the years, particularly among feminist critics.

The first scene that Michael shows Adam, the murder of Abel by Cain followed by the "house of death" is really Adam's introduction to death. Before this scene, Adam has no experience of death. The murder and the grotesque scenes in the "Lazar-house" (479) impress on Adam the monstrosity he has loosed on the world. Also the discussion of grotesque diseases leading to death versus the death of good men, dropping like ripe fruit in old age, seems to suggest that horrible deaths are the result of evil lives. That Milton would suggest this idea seems strange, given his own blindness.

Theme

The last two visions that Michael shows Adam deal first with war and then the destruction of the world by flood. The unifying factor in these two scenes, as well as an image that runs throughout the work, is that of the one good man willing to stand up against a host of opponents. First, Enoch tries to resolve the issues of the war with reason and is nearly killed before God takes him to Heaven. Second, the story of Noah is similar in that Noah alone of the people on Earth speaks out against sin and evil. Eventually, only Noah and his family are saved when the flood comes. Michael explains, "So all shall turn degenerate, all deprav'd, / Justice and Temperance, Truth and Faith forgot; / One Man except, the only Son of light / in a dark Age" (806–809). The examples of Enoch and Noah here recall Abdiel, the only one of Satan's angels who opposed his plan for rebellion. Throughout *Paradise Lost,* the one just man standing up to the evil has been put forward as the example. The Son, accepting mortality and death to save Mankind, is the ultimate paradigm for this image. The image is of particular importance to Adam because he failed to stand up to Eve and, through her, the serpent, in his moment of testing.

Book XI ends with the rainbow, God's covenant with Noah and the one truly hopeful sign in the entire book. For the most part, Michael's description of history has been what most critics call "degenerative history," showing the steady decline of Mankind. This view of the world is similar to the classic myth of the Four Ages of Man in which Mankind goes from a Golden Age, a paradise, through deteriorating stages of Silver, Bronze, and the present Iron, in which ultimate collapse seems imminent. In the *Inferno*, Dante had presented this myth in the image of a statue with a golden head, silver shoulders and chest, bronze torso, and iron legs. Dante added clay feet to symbolize the corruption of the church. *Paradise Lost* and biblical history follow this same pattern to a point. They both begin with paradise in Eden and show successive stages of degeneration until God destroys the world by flood.

The difference between the classic view and Milton's Christian presentation is the rainbow. After Noah finds land, God makes a promise never to destroy the world by fire or flood until sin is burned away for eternity in a final conflagration. Thus, the rainbow represents the hope of salvation for all those who remain obedient to God. The Abdiels, Enochs, Noahs, and, we presume, Adams and Eves will eventually find eternal life because they do not deviate from God's path. The colors of the rainbow provide the Christian contrast with pagan gold, silver, bronze, and iron and offer a sense of optimism at the end of what has been a very grim and depressing presentation of history.

Glossary

prevenient (3)   antecedent to human action.

propitiation (34)   gracious.

Amarantin (78)   dark purplish-red.

descry (228)   to catch sight of; discern.

gripe (264)   [Archaic] to grasp or clutch; to distress; oppress; afflict.

euphrasy (414)   eyebright; any plant of the figwort family having pale lavender flowers in leafy clusters.

rue (414)   an herb with yellow flowers and bitter-tasting leaves.

Lazar-house (479)   a house of the diseased and dying, especially for lepers.

catarrh (483)   inflammation of a mucous membrane, esp. of the nose or throat, causing an increased flow of mucus.

effeminate (634)   having the qualities generally attributed to women; unmanly; not virile. Milton uses the term in the sense that a man allows a woman to take his place in the natural hierarchy in which, for Milton, women were inferior to men, especially in terms of reason and intellect.

Book XII

Summary

Book XII continues Michael's presentation of biblical history to Adam. He begins with the story of Nimrod and the Tower of Babel. Nimrod was known as a great hunter, and Michael adds that men "shall be his game" (30). By this the angel refers to Nimrod's rule over men that ultimately leads him to challenge God through the construction of the Tower of Babel. God stops this enterprise by changing the languages of those constructing the tower so that they cannot work together. Adam is upset that some men have dominion over others. Michael explains that because men cannot control their passions, other men take control of societies. God sends unjust rulers to control some groups so that they lose their personal freedom.

Michael goes on to explain that so many people in the world are wicked that God eventually decides to focus on the Israelites and their faithful leader, Abraham, who carries the seed that will ultimately produce the Savior. Here, Michael moves quickly through the stories of Jacob and Joseph followed by the enslavement of the Israelites in Egypt to the rise of Moses as leader of the great exodus from Egypt. Moses leads the people into the desert, receives the Commandments from God, and begins to establish laws for the people. Adam asks why men need so many laws, to which Michael responds that the need for laws shows the degeneration of people. The laws help men remember to do those things that they should know to do by themselves. Even so, Man cannot truly be saved until Jesus comes to sacrifice himself for all Mankind.

Joshua eventually leads the Israelites to the Promised Land where they set up a society in which they are ruled by judges and kings. The greatest king is David whose lineage will carry the seed of the Savior. David's son, Solomon, will build the great temple to house the Ark of the Covenant. However, later kings will allow such a falling away from God that God will allow the entire nation to fall into captivity in Babylon. Factions in the society will fight among themselves for long periods of time until, under Roman rule, the Messiah will be born to a virgin.

When Adam expresses interest in the coming battle, Michael then explains that the Messiah's victory over Satan will not occur in a literal fight. Instead, the Son will become human in Jesus, will suffer for his beliefs, and will be executed. However, after three days, Jesus will rise from the dead, thereby overcoming Death that Adam loosed upon the world. Jesus will also send out disciples to spread his message to the entire world. Those who obey God's commands will be saved and have eternal life. At the end of time, Jesus will judge the living and the dead, and the truly faithful will enter the most wonderful paradise of all.

Adam is pleased to learn all that Michael has told him, and his greatest pleasure is to have learned that death will actually lead to a great reward. He says that his fall will now become a happy blame, or what some call *felix culpa*. The goodness of God will, through death, provide all Mankind with the chance to live eternally with God. Adam sees this possibility as an even greater good than his having remained sinless in Eden. Michael praises Adam for his reason and tells him to add faith, virtue, patience, temperance, and love to his understanding and he will lead a good life and ultimately be with God.

It is time for the humans to leave Eden. Michael instructs Adam to wake Eve and at a later time tell her all that he has learned from the angel. When Eve is awakened, she says that she has learned much from her dream. She knows that her place is with Adam, and that she will always go where he goes. Further she is comforted, knowing that the Messiah will come from her seed.

Adam and Eve leave Eden. Michael leads them through the Eastern Gate and down to the plain. Behind them they see the flaming sword that protects Eden from intruders. A brand new world lies before them, and they know that God will be with them. Holding hands, they make their way into the world.

Commentary

Book XII appears to be a simple continuation of Book XI, and, in fact, in the first edition of *Paradise Lost*, Books XI and XII were one book. In the second edition, Milton changed his original ten book format to twelve. One of the changes was the division that created Books XI and XII. Biblical scholars in the seventeenth century dated the Creation at 4,000 B.C. and the flood at 2,000 B.C. So Milton divided his original Book X into two 2,000-year sections, each ending with a savior—Noah in Book XI and Jesus in Book XII. He also arranged for a slightly different presentation in each book. Book XI is presented as a series of almost scene-like visions, each complete in itself. Book XII is much more narrative. Michael says that he will now tell the story, and he presents a grand sweep of historical events rather than a scene-by-scene account.

The historical events that Michael narrates in Book XII continue to develop themes and ideas that have run through all of *Paradise Lost*. The first event is the story of Nimrod and the Tower of Babel. Adam's concern about this story is the fact that one man has dominion over others. Adam comments that God gave Man dominion over animals but not over his fellow man. Michael admires Adam's reasoning but shows that domination of man over man is a part of Adam's original sin. When a person allows his reason to be controlled by either his appetite or his will, he reverses the proper order that God intended. God, seeing that Man lets "unworthy powers" (91) rule within himself, then allows tyrants to appear among men and assert authority over them.

Theme

This emphasis of reason as the pre-eminent faculty in Man is one of Milton's main themes in *Paradise Lost*. In the *Inferno*, Dante had divided all sin into three categories: sins of appetite, sins of the will, and sins of reason. The worst sins were those of reason because they perverted the part of man that makes him distinguishable from other creatures. In *Paradise Lost*, Adam and Eve both commit sins of the appetite: she upon eating the apple, he in his passion for Eve above all else. Adam also commits a sin of the will by eating the apple even though his reason tells him to do so is wrong. However, neither Adam nor Eve commits a sin of reason; they are unable to deny seriously any of their actions. Satan commits the sins of reason. His speech to Eve is a perfect example. He uses reason to persuade Eve to eat the apple. By using his reason for fraudulent purposes, he commits what the Middle Ages and Renaissance would have considered to be the worst type of sinful act.

Milton evidently agrees with Dante's ideas of sin, at least in a general way. Throughout the poem, Milton makes reason stand out as the faculty that Man must rely on. In the story of Nimrod, Michael justifies one man's domination over another on Man's inability to keep reason at the forefront in decision making. All the evils that come into the world, whether they involve appetite or will, are really there because of a breakdown of reason.

In the second part of Michael's recounting of history in Book XII, the angel begins to focus on certain heroes within a specific culture—the Israelites. He tells of Abraham, alludes to Jacob and Joseph, presents Moses as a type of savior, and presents the history of the Israeli kings, beginning with Joshua leading the people into the Promised Land followed by accounts of David and Solomon.

Michael explains that God grew weary of the iniquities of the world, and left most nations to "their own polluted ways" (110). He turned his attention instead to "one peculiar Nation" (111), the Israelites, who were to spring from Abraham, a man faithful to God. This account by Michael explains why the Jews (Israelites) were the "Chosen People." God found the faithful man, Abraham, and decided to concentrate his attention on the people and nations that came from that individual. Rather than destroy the rest of the world for its sinfulness, God simply turned away from it to focus on Abraham and his people. Abraham obeys God's commands and goes into Canaan, a land that God promises to all of his future generations. There, Abraham establishes the beginnings of the Kingdom of Israel.

Another important aspect of the selection of Abraham and the Israelites by God is the passage of "the Seed." God had said that the seed of Eve would bruise the serpent, and in Book XII, Michael makes clear that "By that seed / Is meant thy Great Deliverer" (148–49). The "Great Deliverer" is, of course, Jesus, who will come to save Mankind from sin and death. Therefore, Michael's explanation about the Chosen People becomes clearer to Adam. These people, the Israelites, carry the seed of the Messiah; they are chosen initially because of Abraham's godliness, but they are chosen because the Messiah must come from them. Adam begins to see the point of Michael's history lesson.

The nature of this lesson is extended by the humans that Michael chooses to lift up as examples, particularly Moses. The figures of Abraham, Moses, Joshua, and David are all, in varying degrees, prefigurations of Jesus. The practice of "typological allegory or symbolism" began very early in the Christian church. The basis behind this idea was to make the Old Testament more theologically compatible with New Testament for Christians. The general idea was that figures and events in the Old Testaments were types or prefigurations of characters and events in the New Testament. That is, Noah, as the savior of the world in Exodus, prefigures Jesus, the savior of the world in the Gospels. This sort of typological study went beyond the Bible. Classical heroes like Aeneas, Hercules, or Dionysus were sometimes presented as types of Jesus or other important New Testament characters. The justification for this sort of analysis was that God had control of the entire world, and so even in pagan societies, he had provided shadows that pointed the way toward Jesus and Christian belief.

Literary Device

Michael's description of Moses shows Milton's typological intentions. When the Israelites want to know God's will, they ask Moses to be their mediator, a function, which Michael says, "Moses in figure bears, to introduce / One greater of whose day he shall foretell" (241–42). In other words, Moses as mediator with God prefigures Jesus performing the same function in the New Testament. Earlier, Michael has stated the general idea that events and characters inform "by types / And shadows, of that destin'd Seed to bruise / The Serpent, by what means he shall achieve / Mankind's deliverance" (232–35). This statement is very close to a definition for typological symbolism. The characters and events Michael describes are "types and shadows" all pointing toward the Christ of the New Testament. Moses is the most fully explained of these types, but Abraham, Joshua, and David all serve similar functions. The Chosen People carry the seed literally and symbolically that will ultimately bruise the serpent.

Finally, Michael comes to the Savior himself. Here at last, in Michael's description of Jesus and his mission, Adam sees the complete working out of his fall and God's transformation of it. The Son, born of God and the seed of Adam and Eve, becomes Man, takes on Man's sins, and accepts death in order to overcome it. Thereafter, those who believe and accept God's laws will be able to overcome death also. Adam, at last, sees the entirety of God's plan and is exultant. He shouts joyously, "O goodness infinite! goodness immense, / That all this good of evil shall produce, / And evil turn to good" (469–71). Here Adam expresses the idea of the "happy fault" or, in Latin *felix culpa*. If Adam and Eve had not sinned, Jesus would not have been born, Mary would not have been sanctified, and salvation would not have come into existence. These things are greater than what would have existed if the fall had not occurred; therefore, Adam's fall was ultimately for the good.

The idea of the "happy fall" stands in contrast to the more common notion that Adam's action simply created sin and death and destroyed Man's chance for blissful, paradisiacal immortality. Both concepts of the fall existed in seventeenth-century theology, and Milton chooses to accentuate the *felix culpa* as part of his justification of God's ways to Man. By emphasizing the good that will emerge from the fall of Man,

Milton makes the end of *Paradise Lost*, if not triumphant, at least optimistic. Adam and Eve are no longer the beautiful, but strangely aloof, innocents of Books I through VIII. At the end of the epic, as they leave Eden, Adam and Eve are truly human. Their innocence has been transformed by experience, and they now approach the world with a greater knowledge of what can happen and what consequences can follow evil actions. The pride they had in their inability to do evil has been replaced with the knowledge of what evil is and how easy it is to give in to both pride and evil.

In the end, Adam expresses what he has learned from Michael:

Henceforth I learn that to obey is best,
And learn to fear that only God, to walk
As in his presence, ever to observe
His providence, and on him sole depend,
Merciful over all his works, with good
Still overcoming evil, and by small
Accomplishing great things, by things deem'd weak
Subverting worldly strong, and worldly wise
By simple meek; that suffering for Truth's sake
Is fortitude to highest victory,
And to the faithful Death the Gate of Life (561–571).

Theme

This lesson that God is always at work in the world, often through seemingly insignificant people and things, that the greatest heroes are those who suffer for truth, and that death leads to eternal life are the images of hope and possibly triumph at the end of the poem. Adam and Eve go forth at the end with each other—and with God. They know that through obedience, love, and reason, they can live good lives and overcome the evil that they have done. Their knowledge and their hope thus stand as Milton's justification for God's ways.

Glossary

arrogate (27)   to claim or seize without right.

enthrallment (171)   [Now Rare] enslavement.

obdurate (205)   stubborn; obstinate; inflexible.

blasphemed (411)   to have spoken irreverently or profanely of or to God or sacred things.

usurp (421)   to take or assume power, a position, property, rights, etc. and hold in possession by force or without right.

loath (585)   unwilling; reluctant.

marish (630)   [Archaic] a marsh; swamp.

brand (643)   [Archaic] a sword.

CHARACTER ANALYSES

The following character analyses delve into the physical, emotional, and psychological traits of the literary work's major characters so that you might better understand what motivates these characters. The writer of this study guide provides this scholarship as an educational tool by which you may compare your own interpretations of the characters. Before reading the character analyses that follow, consider first writing your own short essays on the characters as an exercise by which you can test your understanding of the original literary work. Then, compare your essays to those that follow, noting discrepancies between the two. If your essays appear lacking, that might indicate that you need to re-read the original literary work or re-familiarize yourself with the major characters.

Satan

Probably, the most famous quote about *Paradise Lost* is William Blake's statement that Milton was "of the Devil's party without knowing it." While Blake may have meant something other than what is generally understood from this quotation (see "Milton's Style" in the Critical Essays), the idea that Satan is the hero, or at least a type of hero, in *Paradise Lost* is widespread. However, the progression, or, more precisely, regression, of Satan's character from Book I through Book X gives a much different and much clearer picture of Milton's attitude toward Satan.

Writers and critics of the Romantic era advanced the notion that Satan was a Promethean hero, pitting himself against an unjust God. Most of these writers based their ideas on the picture of Satan in the first two books of *Paradise Lost*. In those books, Satan rises off the lake of fire and delivers his heroic speech still challenging God. Satan tells the other rebels that they can make "a Heav'n of Hell, a Hell of Heav'n" (I, 255) and adds, "Better to reign in Hell than serve in Heav'n" (I, 263). Satan also calls for and leads the grand council. Finally, he goes forth on his own to cross Chaos and find Earth. Without question, this picture of Satan makes him heroic in his initial introduction to the reader.

Besides his actions, Satan also appears heroic because the first two books focus on Hell and the fallen angels. The reader's introduction to the poem is through Satan's point of view. Milton, by beginning *in medias res* gives Satan the first scene in the poem, a fact that makes Satan the first empathetic character. Also, Milton's writing in these books, and his characterization of Satan, make the archfiend understandable and unforgettable.

These facts certainly make Satan the most interesting character in the poem—but they do not make him the hero. Because the reader hears Satan's version first, the reader is unaware of the exaggerations and outright lies that are parts of Satan's magnificent speeches. Moreover, the reader can easily overlook the fact that Milton states that, whatever powers and abilities the fallen angels have in Hell, those powers and abilities come from God, who could at any moment take them away.

In essence then, Milton's grand poetic style sets Satan up as heroic in Books I and II. The presentation of Satan makes him seem greater than he actually is and initially draws the reader to Satan's viewpoint. Further, because all of the other characters in the poem—Adam, Eve,

God, the Son, the angels—are essentially types rather than characters, Milton spends more artistic energy on the development of Satan so that throughout the poem, Satan's character maintains the reader's interest and, perhaps, sympathy—at least to an extent.

No matter how brilliantly Milton created the character of Satan, the chief demon cannot be the hero of the poem. For Milton, Satan is the enemy who chooses to commit an act that goes against the basic laws of God, that challenges the very nature of the universe. Satan attempts to destroy the hierarchy of Heaven through his rebellion. Satan commits this act not because of the tyranny of God but because he wants what *he* wants rather than what God wants. Satan is an egoist. His interests always turn on his personal desires. Unlike Adam, who discusses a multiplicity of subjects with Raphael, rarely mentioning his own desires, Satan sees everything in terms of what will happen to him. A true Promethean / Romantic hero has to rebel against an unjust tyranny in an attempt to right a wrong or help someone less fortunate. If Satan had been Prometheus, he would have stolen fire to warm himself, not to help Mankind.

Milton shows his own attitude toward Satan in the way the character degenerates or is degraded in the progression of the poem. Satan is magnificent, even admirable in Books I and II. By book IV, he is changed. In his soliloquy that starts Book IV, Satan declares that Hell is wherever he himself is. Away form his followers and allowed some introspection, Satan already reveals a more conflicted character.

Similarly, Satan's motives change as the story advances. At first, Satan wishes to continue the fight for freedom from God. Later his motive for continuing the fight becomes glory and renown. Next, the temptation of Adam and Eve is simply a way to disrupt God's plans. And, at the end, Satan seems to say that he has acted as he has to impress the other demons in Hell. This regression of motives shows quite a fall.

Satan also regresses or degenerates physically. Satan shifts shapes throughout the poem. These changes visually represent the degeneration of his character. First, he takes the form of a lesser angel, a cherub, when he speaks to Uriel. Next, he is a ravening cormorant in the tree of life—an animal but able to fly. Then he is a lion and a tiger—earthbound beasts of prey, but magnificent. Finally, he is a toad and a snake. He becomes reptilian and disgusting. These shape changes graphically reveal how Satan's actions change him.

Even in his own shape, Satan degenerates. When Gabriel confronts Satan in Book V, none of the angels initially recognize Satan because his appearance is noticeably changed. Likewise, in Book X, when Satan once again sits on his throne in Hell, none of the earlier magnificence of his physical appearance is left. Now he looks like a drunken debauchee.

Though Satan is not heroic in *Paradise Lost*, he at times does border on tragedy. Ironically, he also borders on comedy. The comic element associated with Satan derives from the absurdity of his position. As a rebel, he challenges an omnipotent foe, God, with power that is granted him by his foe. God simply toys with Satan in battle. Satan is, in fact, cartoonish when he and Belial gloat over the success of their infernal cannon in Book VI. Satan and Belial stand laughing at the disorder they have caused, but they are unaware of the mountains and boulders just about to land on their heads.

If all of *Paradise Lost* were on the level of the battle scene, the poem would be comic. But Satan's temptation of Adam and Eve moves the demon closer to tragedy. Satan's motives in destroying the human couple may be arguable, but the effect and its implications are not. Satan brings the humans down and causes their removal from Eden. In so doing, he also provides the way to salvation for those humans who choose freely to obey God. However, Satan provides nothing for himself. Hell is where Satan is because he has no way to rejoin God. Unlike humanity, Satan and the other fallen angels have already sealed their fates. They live always with the knowledge of Hell.

In the end, Satan calls to mind the Macbeth of Shakespeare. Both characters are magnificent creations of evil. Both are heroic after a fashion, but both are doomed. Both are fatalistic about the afterlife. Satan knows that he must remain in Hell; Macbeth says that he would "jump the life to come," if he could kill Duncan with no consequence on Earth. Both characters are the driving force in their own works. And finally both create a kind of Hell; Macbeth's on Earth, Satan's in the universe.

God

Because God created the Son, the angels, Man, Heaven, Earth, and everything else, and since he is omniscient, Milton was faced with the difficulty of creating tension about what would happen since God already knew. This problem, of course, existed in one way or another in most Greek epics and tragedies so that the real question was in the presentation of a known set of incidents. Milton approaches the problem of God's character by making him almost a chorus-like figure. God comments on scenes and actions, he explains what will happen and why, he gives the philosophical / theological basis for ideas like free will, but he does not truly participate in the action.

God is aloof, almost emotionless. He embodies pure reason, and consequently his responses often seem cold. In the war in Heaven, God limits the power of the faithful angels and in the final moments sends only the Son to conquer the rebels. Yet his cosmic laugh at the presumption of Satan and his crew has a chilling effect. If the reader had had any doubts about Satan's power against God, that laugh puts them to rest.

God's unemotional reason is not without another side. God is also pure justice. He may see his plans for Man dashed by Satan's trickery, but through divine justice, he will put everything to right and conquer Satan. From evil, God will produce goodness. God gave Man free will. From Man's free will, sin and death came into the world, but God will see that goodness rules in the end.

The Son

The merciful, compassionate side of God is presented in the Son, not referred to as Jesus because Jesus had not been born at this time in theological history. In Book III, God says that Adam and Eve will fall and must suffer death. However, death can be overcome for humans if someone in Heaven will sacrifice himself to death for Man. The Son says that he will become human and die in order to defeat death. This act clearly defines the Son. He is powerful and brave, merciful, and willing to act to help Mankind. God's duty is to provide justice—the law has been declared. It is the Son who provides mercy to temper justice— the natural law.

The Son's power is also further revealed in Book VI when God decides to end the rebellion of the angels. God sends only the Son in a chariot against Satan and his hosts. The Son by himself is able to defeat the rebellious angels and cast them into Hell. Milton uses the Son as the acting hand of God's decisions.

God also uses the Son as the creator of Earth and the universe around it. Milton connects the Son closely to Mankind by making the

Son the creator of the biblical account. Even though Milton refers to the Son as God in Book VII, it is, nonetheless, the Son who, with golden compasses, lays out the universe and creates Earth and Mankind. Once again, the Son carries out God's plan.

Finally, after the fall of Adam and Eve, the Son goes to Earth at God's request and passes judgment on the serpent, Adam, and Eve. Beyond telling the humans what their punishment will be, the Son also pities them and clothes them in skins. God seems to be almost the embodiment of ideas while the Son converts those ideas to actions.

At the end of *Paradise Lost*, Michael shows Adam a vision of Jesus, who is the Seed that will ultimately destroy Satan. This scene is the obvious close of the story. The Son, becoming human through Jesus, will live and die. Through resurrection from death, he will finally overcome Satan and save man from the results of the fall. If the reader finds God difficult to comprehend, he finds the Son more compassionate and merciful. Through both characters combined, Milton presents a complete picture of God.

Adam

Before the fall, Adam is as nearly perfect a human being as can be imagined. He is physically attractive, mentally adept, and spiritually profound. He stands out in Eden as the apex of the hierarchical pyramid. Only Eve can compare to him, and she only in physical beauty.

The conversations between Adam and Eve before Book X are models of civilized discourse. These conversations are difficult to imagine as real, but they reflect the nature of the two humans. Adam's and humanity's values are reflected in his attitude, which is revealed through his speech—to Eve, to Raphael, and to God. In each instance when Adam speaks, he shows the proper relationship to the being with whom he converses. While he is superior to Eve and inferior to Raphael and God, there is still no hint of haughtiness in his discussions with Eve or of subservience in his talks with the angel and God. Always Adam shows the proper respect and relationship in graceful speech and manners.

When Adam sees Raphael's approach to Earth, he tells Eve, "go with speed, / And what thy stores contain, bring forth and pour / Abundance, fit to honor and receive / Our Heav'nly stranger" (V, 313–316). Eve replies, "Adam, earth's hallowed mould, / Of God inspir'd, small store will serve, where store, / All seasons, ripe for use hangs on the stalk"

(V, 321–323). These words, which may seem overly formal, nonetheless reveal the relationship of Adam and Eve. Adam is in charge, but his request for Eve to prepare a meal is not a dismissive command. Likewise, her response shows that she knows more about the food situation in Eden than Adam. This brief dialogue is a discussion between near equals who understand their responsibilities to each other and to the world.

Adam's conversation with Raphael is similar and marked by the same tone. Adam welcomes Raphael graciously but in a manner that acknowledges the superior standing of the angel. Further, Adam uses his time with the angel to learn about Heaven, about angels, about the war in Heaven, about creation, and about astronomy. Adam's curiosity and intellect are revealed. Likewise, Adam informs Raphael about Adam's and Eve's creation and about their relationship. Man and Angel have information for each other, and they present this information within the formalized structure that establishes their relationship.

After Adam's fall, his conversations with Eve become querulous. He blames her, and she him. It takes a *mea culpa* speech by Eve to rekindle Adam's love for his wife and to reestablish their proper relationship. Likewise, when Michael comes to Eden, the relationship between Man and Angel has changed. Michael is stern but compassionate. He presents the vision of the future to Adam, but there is little, if any, give and take between the two. Adam and Raphael have a social meeting in which hierarchy is understood. Michael and Adam have a hierarchical meeting in which Michael talks and Adam listens.

If Adam has a flaw before the fall, it is uxoriousness. This term, which means "dotingly or irrationally fond of or submissive to one's wife," was applied to Adam early on in criticism of *Paradise Lost*. Adam tells Raphael that Eve's beauty affects him so much "that what she wills to do or say, / Seems wisest, virtuosest, discreetest, best; / All higher knowledge in her presence falls / Degraded" (VIII, 549–552). Even though Raphael warns Adam that this attitude toward Eve is improper and that Satan could use it to tempt the humans, Adam eats the fruit of the Tree of Knowledge precisely because he cannot bear to be without Eve. As a near perfect human, Adam is ruled by reason. He immediately understands Eve's sin in eating the apple, but he willfully ignores his reason and eats because of his love and desire for her. Adam's uxorious attitude toward Eve, which perverts the hierarchy of Earth and Paradise, leads directly to his fall.

After the fall, Adam is prey to self-doubt, to anger and sullenness, and to self-pity. Ironically, Eve's love for him starts Adam on the path back to righteousness. Adam, after the fall, will never again be the old Adam, but he does recover his reason, he develops a new understanding of and love for Eve, and he sees the good that God will produce from his and Eve's sinful action. Adam goes from being the perfect human to becoming a good human.

Eve

Eve is a simpler character than Adam. She is created from Adam's rib as his helpmeet. While she is beautiful, wise, and able, she is superior to Adam only in her beauty. From the time of her creation, when she looks in the water and falls in love with her own reflection, Eve is linked to the flaw of vanity, and Satan as the serpent will use this defect against her.

Before the fall, Eve is generally presented as submissive to Adam and, to some extent, dependent on him. Her reasoning powers are not as fully realized as his. However, Milton in no way suggests a lack of intelligence on Eve's part. Eve listens to Raphael's description of the war in Heaven and the defeat of the rebellious angels. When the conversation turns to more abstract questions of creation and planetary motion at the start of Book VIII, Eve walks away to tend her Garden. Milton is quick to note, however, "Yet went she not, as not with such discourse / Delighted, or not capable of her ear / Of what was high: such pleasures she reserv'd, / Adam relating, she sole Auditress" (VIII, 48–51). In other words, Eve is perfectly capable of comprehending the abstruse subject, but she prefers hearing the ideas from Adam alone. The implied idea here is that Eve understands her position in the hierarchical arrangement and leaves this conversation so that she will in no way usurp Adam's place with the angel.

Eve does have a tendency now and then to question Adam, but she does so in a rational, respectful manner. In Book IX, such questioning leads to temptation. Eve tell Adam at the start of Book IX that they can do more work if they work separately. Adam knows that Eve is more likely to be tricked by Satan if she is alone and argues against separation. His love for Eve, though, allows him to be persuaded, and against his better judgment, he lets her go. Most commentators see this action on Adam's part as another example of his uxoriousness; he yields to Eve's argument, not because her argument is better, but because he does not want to hurt her feelings. On the other hand, Eve wins the argument by knowingly using her advantages over Adam. Eve sets herself up for the fall and is not equal to the task of dealing with Satan by herself.

Eve yields to temptation through a combination of flattery (vanity) and sophistic argument by the serpent. Satan is happy to find Eve alone and acknowledges that Adam would be a much more difficult opponent. Satan knows Eve's weaknesses and plays on them. She is charmed by him and cannot detect the flaws in his arguments.

After she eats the fruit, Eve immediately changes. She begins to think of ways of becoming Adam's equal or perhaps his superior. But, fearful of losing Adam to another female creation, she decides that he must eat the fruit also. Adam does so but not because of Eve's arguments. He eats willfully because he is unwilling to be parted from Eve.

After the fall, Eve, like Adam, is acrimonious and depressed. However, her love for Adam initiates the regeneration of the pair. She apologizes, and her love causes a change in Adam; they can face the future together. Eve is also glorified by being told that her seed will eventually destroy Satan, though her position in relation to Adam is made clear when Michael puts her to sleep while he shows Adam the vision of the future.

Eve is certainly not a feminist heroine. Like so many characters in the epic, she has an assigned role in the hierarchy of the universe. Milton does not denigrate women through the character of Eve; he simply follows the thought of his time as to the role of women in society. Eve has as many important responsibilities as Adam, but in the hierarchy of the universe, she falls just below him.

CRITICAL ESSAYS

On the pages that follow, the writer of this study guide provides critical scholarship on various aspects of Milton's *Paradise Lost*. These interpretive essays are intended solely to enhance your understanding of the original literary work; they are supplemental materials and are not to replace your reading of *Paradise Lost*. When you're finished reading *Paradise Lost*, and prior to your reading this study guide's critical essays, consider making a bulleted list of what you think are the most important themes and symbols. Write a short paragraph under each bullet explaining why you think that theme or symbol is important; include at least one short quote from the original literary work that supports your contention. Then, test your list and reasons against those found in the following essays. Do you include themes and symbols that the study guide author doesn't? If so, this self test might indicate that you are well on your way to understanding original literary work. But if not, perhaps you will need to re-read *Paradise Lost*.

Milton's Universe

The universe, including Heaven and Hell, that Milton imagines in *Paradise Lost* was much more familiar to his original audience than to today's readers. Today the heliocentric view of the solar system and many more, at times baffling, theories about the universe and its creation are accepted without question. In seventeenth-century England, the debate between the geocentric view of the universe, proposed by the ancient Roman astronomer, Ptolemy, and the heliocentric view, advocated by Copernicus, Kepler, Brahe, Galileo, and others was still fiercely debated.

Through the years, critics have argued confidently about Milton's view of this debate, though these same critics have often been in disagreement concerning which side Milton accepted. Evidence exists that Milton might have met Galileo. Milton mentions Galileo's telescope in the poem (V, 262–62). But, when Adam asks Raphael whether the Earth is stationary with the rest of the universe circling it or whether the Earth circles the sun along with the other planets, Raphael (and Milton) equivocates, leaving Milton's own views unstated.

Of course, the geocentric / heliocentric debate is but one small part of the cosmos that Milton presents in *Paradise Lost*. In general terms, Milton describes a universe with Heaven at the top, Hell at the bottom, and Chaos in between. Earth dangles on a golden chain dropped from Heaven, and, by the end of the epic, a bridge connects Hell to Earth. To grasp the significance of this view of the universe, one must examine each part separately and compare the fictional / theological construct with the scientific knowledge of Milton's day.

Heaven

At the top of the universe is Heaven. It is inhabited by God and those angels who did not rebel against him. The primary quality of Heaven is light. God is pure light of such quality that the angels must observe him through a cloud. The angels themselves are also a type of stunning, pure light but not comparable to the light of God because they give off colors. Raphael is described as being made of "colors dipt in Heaven" (283) in Book V. Milton's source for this Heaven of light is the first command of God in Genesis: "'Let there be light' and there was light."

The name Milton uses for this light-filled Heaven is the Empyrean, which for classical authors was the indestructible realm of light or fire.

Thus, when the war in Heaven occurs, it is between beings who are indestructible. God says that the rebellious angels can be annihilated, but exactly what he means is never clear. With that one exception, however, everything associated with Heaven or the Empyrean is eternal and indestructible.

Within Heaven, God sits at the top of a mountain on his eternal throne. He is shrouded in a cloudy mist because of the quality and intensity of the light he emanates. The Son is at his side. In orthodox Protestant theology, they are two parts of a tripartite whole—the Holy Spirit being the third. Each of these characters represents an aspect of God. God is the Father; pure reason and intellect, perfect unemotional justice. The Son is the more merciful side. He demonstrates pity, mercy, sacrifice, and hope. (The Holy Spirit is mentioned only in the prologues as the true Urania, Milton's muse.) In Milton's personal view, the Son and God are not the same. God created the Son who is so close to God that any distinction is imperceptible, even to angelic sensibilities. Theologically then, Milton was a Unitarian, though he never develops this viewpoint in *Paradise Lost*.

Below God and the Son are the angels. Traditional Christian thought grouped angels into nine hierarchical categories. The traditional Christian categories and hierarchies of angels were Seraphim, Cherubim, Thrones, Dominations or Dominions, Virtues, Powers, Principalities, Archangels, and Angels. Milton mentions all of these groups in *Paradise Lost*, but he does not adhere strictly to the hierarchies. Each of these classifications was called a choir. Each group of three choirs starting at the top with Seraphim, Cherubim, and Thrones had specific functions in relation to God.

It is readily apparent that Milton does not follow this arrangement of angels in his depiction of Heaven. The important angels—Michael, Raphael, Gabriel—are called archangels and certainly seem to be those closest to God. Further, when Satan approaches the archangel Uriel on the sun in Book III, he disguises himself as a cherubim, a "stripling Cherub" (636), obviously of lesser rank than Uriel. Moreover, Satan addresses Uriel as a "Seraph" (667), which is a confusion of two highly separated categories.

Milton's attitude toward the angels is at best hazy. Most of the time, he seems to follow the ancient Hebrew tradition that classified all angels as either angels or archangels, with the archangels being the more important and the closest to God. However, Milton also mentions all the other categories in several places. In the end, the only real conclusion is that with angels, as with so many other aspects of *Paradise Lost*, Milton follows his own ideas while maintaining at least the semblance of the traditional Christian doctrine and emphasizing the hierarchy. He acknowledges the hierarchy of angels but arranges it to suit his own views.

Hell

Hell in *Paradise Lost* is the antithesis of Heaven. In a sense, Hell is an ironic parody of Heaven. Hell for Milton is literally the underworld. Heaven is the zenith of the universe, then there is the great gulf of Chaos and Night, and finally, at the bottom, underneath everything, is Hell.

The phrase associated with Milton's Hell that has occasioned much discussion is the statement that Hell, "As one great furnace flamed, yet from those flames / No light, but rather, darkness visible" (I, 62–63). The idea of flames that do give off light and darkness that is visible has troubled some commentators over the years. But, while one may grant that the phrase "darkness visible" is oxymoronic, it is also meaningful. Heaven, which is pure light, is also pure goodness. Hell is the opposite, pure evil and pure darkness, in fact a darkness so pure that it is visible, a contrasting quality to the blinding light of Heaven.

At first, Hell seems like Dante's place of miserable torment. The fallen angels wake, lying on a lake of fire, surrounded by sulfurous fumes. However, this first image of Hell is soon replaced by a second. The demons build a capital, Pandemonium, with a palace and a throne for Satan, contrasting with God's throne in Heaven. The demons also have contests, sing, and debate, so that Hell begins to seem more like Dante's Limbo, not such bad place except that it is apart from God. Both these images are aspects of Hell for Milton; it is a place of punishment and also a place where demons live in a manner that ironically imitates Heaven. The difference is that the demons' games, songs, and debates are all corrupt and have no true end unlike the absolute beauty and truth of Heaven.

Milton will also introduce a third Hell, an inner, psychological Hell. At the start of Book IV, Satan has a soliloquy in which he concludes, "Which way I fly is Hell; myself am Hell" (75). This inner Hell is as much a part of Milton's universe as the physical lake of fire. In fact, for Milton, the inner turmoil that makes anywhere Satan is into Hell is probably the foremost Hell. Hell as a spiritual state that cannot be avoided is worse than any particular place.

In the physical Hell, though, the demons form a hierarchy of sorts. Milton lists no classifications of demons, but obviously some are more important that others. The demons who speak at the council are the most important and ironically match the archangels associated with God. Beelzebub, Belial, Moloch, and Mammon are the chief demons under Satan.

Besides these four demons who speak at the great council, Milton catalogs over a dozen more. Some of the names are familiar; some not. Osiris, Isis, perhaps Baal and Astaroth are recognizable names; Rimnon, Thammuz, Chemos, Dagon, and a number of others are known primarily by scholars. Milton has taken the names of numerous pagan gods who were worshiped by tribes that opposed the Israelites and made them into fallen angels, now demons. For an audience closer to the Bible and biblical literature than a modern one, all of these names resonated with meaning. Milton's point is that the pagan gods were once angels who, in corrupted form, became the false gods of those nations that opposed the Chosen People.

The purpose behind the cataloging of demons in Hell and the hierarchy of angels in Heaven is not made clear by Milton, but the two groups are obviously comparable and intended to be so. Similarly, the different aspects of Hell are usually set up in an ironic contrast with a counterpoint in Heaven. The hierarchy of Hell is not a real arrangement based on superiority and inferiority. Satan has taken control, but in actuality all the fallen angels are essentially the same, a point made clear when they are all turned into snakes and both their importance in the universe and their degrees in Hell vanish. In Heaven, the hierarchy is real; in Hell, a sham.

Chaos

At the top of Milton's universe is Heaven with God on his throne; at the bottom of this universe is Hell, with Satan on his throne. In between the two is Chaos with his consort Night. Chaos and Night are depicted as characters, but they are actually personifications of the great unorganized chasm that separates Heaven from Hell. For Milton, relying on earlier writers and thinkers, Chaos was the formless void that existed before creation. It was the abyss, the darkness, and the mighty wind out of which God created first Heaven and, later, Earth.

Chaos also physically demonstrates the profound width of the gap between Heaven and Hell. Not only is Hell at the bottom of the universe in Milton's design, it is at the bottom of an almost limitless and unimaginably disordered space. Milton describes Chaos as "Eternal Anarchy" (II, 896) and a "wild Abyss" (II, 917). He adds that it is "The Womb of nature, and perhaps her Grave, / Of neither Sea, nor Shore, nor Air, nor Fire, / But all these in their pregnant causes mixt / Confusedly, and which thus must ever fight" (II, 911–914).

In *Paradise Lost*, Satan has to journey across Chaos to find Earth. This journey is long and arduous and is one of the accomplishments of Satan that makes him seem heroic. In Book II, Satan, with no clear idea of where he is going or how to get there, sets out across Chaos, intent on finding God's new creation. If the reader forgets Satan's motive, to corrupt and destroy, then Satan becomes the heroic individual, pitting himself against the universe.

Earth

The Earth that is depicted in *Paradise Lost* is different from the Earth we know today. Milton describes Earth as a creation by God after the rebellion of Satan and his followers. Raphael tells Adam that God created Earth through the Son to keep Satan from feeling pride that he had "dispeopl'd Heav'n" (151). Earth and Man were created so that Man, through trial, could reach the state of the angels, and Earth could become a part of Heaven. To that end, the Son creates not only Earth but also the heavens surrounding Earth, and all that lives on Earth. All of these, he suspends from Heaven on a golden chain. The great image in *Paradise Lost* is of the Son, a celestial architect with a golden compass, plotting out the universe in which Earth will exist.

After its creation, Earth, like Heaven and Hell, has a hierarchical arrangement. Also like Heaven and Hell, this arrangement is understated and vague. On Earth, Paradise—the Garden of Eden—is the paramount place. The hill from which Adam receives his vision of the future from Michael is apparently, though this is not stated, the highest place on Earth. So when Adam and Eve are banished from the Garden, they leave the perfect place on Earth and enter a world that is both flawed and unknown.

On Earth, Adam is the superior being. He was created first, and Eve was created from his rib. Adam is also the paradigmatic Man, the pattern for all who will come later; likewise Eve is the pattern for all women. But, in relation to each other, Adam is superior both in intellect and ability. Eve is more beautiful, but she has been created as a slightly inferior helpmeet to Adam.

Together the two humans are superior to all other living creatures on Earth. Raphael's speech beginning at line 469 in Book V makes it clear that all of the creatures of Earth can be arranged in hierarchical order. The idea that the entire universe is hierarchical was basic to all thought in the seventeenth century. The first serious expressions of the equality of man were still over a century away.

The position of Earth in Milton's universe also reflects a hierarchical arrangement. Heaven is the top of the universe; Hell, the bottom. Earth is attached to Heaven by a golden chain. Had Adam and Eve not fallen, there is a sense that at least metaphorically the chain would have slowly pulled Earth up to Heaven so the two places could merge. The fall changed the nature of the original plan. The fall, however, did not change the connection of Earth to Heaven. The chain remains, although at the end of *Paradise Lost*, a wide bridge across Chaos connects Hell to Earth. Man must either find the difficult way up the chain or stroll across the wide causeway to Hell. The easier pathway is obvious.

The final aspect of Earth in Milton's universe is its position in relation to the scientific knowledge of the day. As noted, Milton was well aware of the scientific theories of his time. He certainly knew the Copernican heliocentric theories and probably accepted them. As with so many specifics in *Paradise Lost,* though, Milton's description of Earth does not reveal his personal views of the geocentric / heliocentric controversy. The chain that attaches Earth to Heaven attaches not only Earth but also the heavens that surround Earth. The universe humans see in the night sky is only a small part, removed by God from the gigantic Chaos which surrounds Earth. Adam's question concerning whether the chain connects to Earth with the sun and stars rotating around the planet or whether the chain attaches in some other way so that Earth rotates around the sun is never answered. Raphael simply says that some questions are better left unanswered, and that God laughs at Man's attempts to understand how he made the universe.

Milton's refusal to give a straight answer to the geocentric / heliocentric debate may have a better rationale behind it than simple bet hedging. Milton consciously wrote *Paradise Lost* for the ages. He saw it as the great Christian epic following in the tradition of Homer, Virgil, Dante, and Tasso. The scientific questions concerning the universe were questions still hotly debated in Milton's time. If Milton had had Raphael explain exactly what God had done, and then, at some later date, that explanation was shown to be false, a serious flaw would exist in *Paradise Lost*—God would be incorrect. By having Raphael equivocate on the answer, Milton allows God to be eternally correct. God knows how he created the universe and how the solar system works, but he does not share that information with Man in *Paradise Lost*.

In the end, Milton's cosmos is one of the great imaginary cosmographies of Western literature. Almost as many depictions of Milton's cosmos exist as do of Dante's Hell, Purgatory, and Heaven. It is a fictional world that presumes to represent the real world. As such, it is an achievement that is almost as impressive as the epic for which it was created.

Major Themes in *Paradise Lost*

Modern criticism of *Paradise Lost* has taken many different views of Milton's ideas in the poem. One problem is that *Paradise Lost* is almost militantly Christian in an age that now seeks out diverse viewpoints and admires the man who stands forth against the accepted view. Milton's religious views reflect the time in which he lived and the church to which he belonged. He was not always completely orthodox in his ideas, but he was devout. His purpose or theme in *Paradise Lost* is relatively easy to see, if not to accept.

Milton begins *Paradise Lost* by saying that he will sing, "Of Man's First Disobedience" (I, 1) so that he can "assert Eternal Providence, / And justify the ways of God to men" (I, 25–26). The purpose or theme of *Paradise Lost* then is religious and has three parts: 1) disobedience, 2) Eternal Providence, and 3) justification of God to men. Frequently, discussions of *Paradise Lost* center on the latter of these three to the exclusion of the first two. And, just as frequently, readers and those casually acquainted with *Paradise Lost* misunderstand what Milton means by the word *justify*, assuming that Milton is rather arrogantly asserting that God's actions and motives seem so arbitrary that they require vindication and explanation.

However, Milton's idea of justification is not as arrogant as many readers think. Milton does not use the word *justification* in its modern sense of proving that an action is or was proper. Such a reading of *justify* would mean that Milton is taking it upon himself to explain the propriety of God's actions—a presumptuous undertaking when one is dealing with any deity. Rather, Milton uses *justify* in the sense of showing the justice that underlies an action. Milton wishes to show that the fall, death, and salvation are all acts of a just God. To understand the theme of *Paradise Lost* then, a reader does not have to accept Milton's ideas as a vindication of God's actions; rather the reader needs to understand the idea of justice that lies behind the actions.

Disobedience

The first part of Milton's argument hinges on the word *disobedience* and its opposite, *obedience.* The universe that Milton imagined with Heaven at the top, Hell at the bottom, and Earth in between is a hierarchical place. God literally sits on a throne at the top of Heaven. Angels are arranged in groups according to their proximity to God. On Earth, Adam is superior to Eve; humans rule over animals. Even in Hell, Satan sits on a throne, higher than the other demons.

This hierarchical arrangement by Milton is not simply happenstance. The worldview of the Middle Ages, Renaissance, and Restoration was that all of creation was arranged in various hierarchies. The proper way of the world was for inferiors to obey superiors because superiors were, well, superior. A king was king not because he was chosen but because he was superior to his subjects. It was, therefore, not just proper to obey the king; it was morally required. Conversely, if the king proved unfit or not superior to his subjects, it was morally improper to obey him and revolution could be justified.

God, being God, was by definition superior to every other thing in the universe and should always be obeyed. In *Paradise Lost,* God places one prohibition on Adam and Eve—not to eat from the Tree of Knowledge. The prohibition is not so much a matter of the fruit of the tree as it is obeying God's ordinance. The proper running of the universe requires the obedience of inferiors to their superiors. By not obeying God's rule, Adam and Eve bring calamity into their lives and the lives of all mankind.

The significance of obedience to superiors is not just a matter of Adam and Eve and the Tree of Knowledge; it is a major subject throughout the poem. Satan's rebellion because of jealousy is the first great act of disobedience and commences all that happens in the epic. When Abdiel stands up to Satan in Book V, Abdiel says that God created the angels "in their bright degrees" (838) and adds "His laws our laws" (844). Abdiel's point is that Satan's rebellion because of the Son is wrong because Satan is disobeying a decree of his obvious superior. Satan has no answer to this point except sophistic rigmarole.

Further instances of the crucial importance of both hierarchy and obedience occur in both large and small matters. The deference with which Adam greets Raphael shows the human accepting his position in regard to the angel. The image is one of the proper manners between inferior and superior. Eve's normal attitude toward Adam reflects the same relationship.

The crucial moment in the poem results from disobedience and a breakdown of hierarchy. Eve argues with Adam about whether they should work together or apart, and Adam gives in to her. The problem here lies with both humans. Eve should not argue with her superior, Adam, but likewise, Adam, should not yield his authority to his inferior, Eve.

When Eve eats the fruit, one of her first thoughts is that the fruit "may render me more equal" (IX, 823) to which she quickly adds, "for inferior who is free?" (IX, 826). Her reasoning, from Milton's point of view, is incorrect. Freedom comes precisely from recognizing one's place in the grand scheme and obeying the dictates of that position. By disobeying God, Eve has gained neither equality nor freedom; she has instead lost Paradise and brought sin and death into the world.

Likewise, when Adam also eats the fruit, he disobeys God. Further, he disobeys by *knowingly* putting Eve ahead of God. Disobedience and disruption of the correct order result in sin and death.

Finally, in the last two books of the epic, Milton shows example after example of people who ignore the responsibilities they have and try to either raise themselves above God or disobey God's commands. The result is always the same—destruction.

The first part of Milton's purpose in *Paradise Lost* then is to show that disobedience leads to a breakdown of hierarchical or social order with disastrous consequences. Some have argued that Milton puts himself in a contradictory position in *Paradise Lost*, since he supported the overthrow of Charles I. In his political writings, Milton makes it clear that obeying an inferior is equally as bad as disobeying a superior. In the case of a king, the people must determine if the king is truly their superior or not. Thus, Milton justifies his position toward Charles and toward God.

Eternal Providence

Milton's theme in *Paradise Lost*, however, does not end with the idea of disobedience. Milton says that he will also "assert Eternal Providence." If Man had never disobeyed God, death would never have entered the world and Man would have become a kind of lesser angel. Because Adam and Eve gave in to temptation and disobeyed God, they provided the opportunity for God to show love, mercy, and grace so that ultimately the fall produces a greater good than would have happened otherwise. This is the argument about the fall called *felix culpa* or "happy fault."

The general reasoning is that God created Man after the rebellion of Satan. His stated purpose is to show Satan that the rebellious angels will not be missed, that God can create new beings as he sees fit. God gives Man a free will, but at the same time, God being God, knows what Man will do because of free will. Over and over in *Paradise Lost*, God says that Man has free will, that God knows Man will yield to Satan's temptation, but that he (God) is not the cause of that yielding; He simply knows that it will occur.

This point is theologically tricky. In many ways, it makes God seem like a cosmic prig. He knows what Man will do, but he does nothing to stop him because somehow that would be against the rules. He could send Raphael with a more explicit warning; he could tell Gabriel and the other guards where Satan will enter Eden; he could seal Satan up in Hell immediately. He could do a number of things to prevent the fall, but he does nothing.

From the standpoint of fictional drama, a reader may be correct in faulting God for the fall of Adam and Eve. From a theological / philosophical standpoint, God *must not* act. If Man truly has free will, he must be allowed to exercise it. Because of free will then, Adam and Eve disobey God and pervert the natural hierarchy. Death is the result, and Death could be the end of the story if *Paradise Lost* were a tragedy.

Justification of God's Ways

Eternal Providence moves the story to a different level. Death must come into the world, but the Son steps forward with the offer to sacrifice himself to Death in order to defeat Death. Through the Son, God is able to temper divine justice with mercy, grace, and salvation. Without the fall, this divine love would never have been demonstrated. Because Adam and Eve disobeyed God, mercy, grace, and salvation occur through God's love, and all Mankind, by obeying God, can achieve salvation. The fall actually produces a new and higher love from God to Man.

This idea then is the final point of Milton's theme—the sacrifice of the Son which overcomes Death gives Man the chance to achieve salvation even though, through the sin of Adam and Eve, all men are sinful. As Adam says, "O goodness infinite, goodness immense! / That all this good of evil shall produce, / And evil turn to good" (XII, 469–471). The fall of Man, then, turns evil into good, and that fact shows the justice of God's actions, or in Milton's terms, "justifies the ways of God to men."

Milton's Grand Style

In the twentieth century, Milton's style first received general criticism from T. S. Eliot. Eliot praised Milton in "A Note on the Verse of John Milton" (Martz 12–18): "[W]hat he could do well he did better than anyone else has ever done." Then Eliot added, "Milton's poetry could only be an influence for the worse, upon any poet whatever." The general thrust of Eliot's criticism is that Milton's purposely adopted grand style is both so difficult to accomplish and so complicated (in places) to understand that it causes a deterioration in the poetic style of those who are influenced by it and cannot meet its demands. "In fact," said Eliot, "it was an influence against which we still have to struggle."

Eliot's prime example is from Book V as Satan addresses his followers concerning the Son:

> Thrones, Dominations, Princedoms, Virtues, Powers,
> If these magnific Titles yet remain
> Not merely titular, since by Decree
> Another now hath to himself ingross't
> All Power, and us eclipst under the name
> Of King anointed, for whom all this haste

Of midnight march, and hurried meeting here,
This only to consult how we may best
With what may be devis'd of honors new
Receive him coming to receive from us
Knee-tribute yet unpaid, prostration vile,
Too much to one, but double how endur'd,
To one and to his image now proclaim'd? (V, 772-784).

That Satan's point here is obscured by the language cannot be denied. Most readers are probably unaware that a question is being asked until they see the question mark at the end of the passage. The meaning here can be puzzled out, but it is difficult to call such writing good, let alone great. Many readers, from put-upon high schoolers to experienced scholars took Eliot's criticism to heart. Often, they overlooked the fact that Eliot did not suggest that Milton was a bad poet; rather he suggested that the grand style could lead to bad poetry, particularly by the many who used Milton's style as the paradigm of great English poetry.

Defenders of Milton quickly appeared to answer Eliot. C. S. Lewis, in his work *A Preface to Paradise Lost,* and Christopher Ricks in *Milton's Grand Style* both mounted vigorous defenses of Milton's style. Lewis in particular argued that Milton needed this particular style for a "secondary epic," his term for an epic meant to be read rather than the "primary epic," which was presented orally in a formal setting and meant to be heard. Lewis' basic point was that the grand style provided the formality of setting that the secondary epic, by the nature of its composition, lost.

Both Lewis and Ricks offered numerous counter examples to show that Milton's style was sublime. Certainly, aside from Shakespeare, no other writer in English could manipulate the language as Milton did. His justly famous description of Mulciber falling soars:

from Morn
To Noon he fell, from Noon to dewy Eve,
A Summer's day; and with the setting Sun
Dropt from the Zenith like a falling Star (I, 742–745).

Or consider the pathos, poignancy, and hopefulness that fill the last few lines of the epic:

Some natural tears they dropped, but wiped them soon;
The world was all before them, where to choose

Their place of rest, and Providence their guide.
They hand in hand, with wand'ring steps and slow,
Through Eden took their solitary way. (XII, 645–650)

However, the questions about Milton's style cannot be answered by playing a game of bad line versus good line. The answer to the question posed by Eliot and opposed by Lewis and Ricks is of such a subjective nature that it can never be truly settled. Arguments about Milton's style will persist just as they do about the styles of Henry James, Jane Austen, even James Joyce. One man's sublimity is another's conundrum.

What *can* be accomplished is a clear description regarding what Milton's grand style consists of and how he made use of it in the poem. With this information, the reader can at least have an objective foundation on which to base his subjective opinion.

Allusions and Vocabulary

The first aspect of the grand style that most readers notice is the number of allusions and references, many of which seem obscure, along with the arcane and archaic vocabulary. In just the first few lines of the poem references to "Oreb" (7), "That Shepherd" (8), "chosen seed" (8), "Siloa's Brook" (10), and "Aonian Mount" (15) occur. The purpose of the references is to extend the reader's understanding through comparison. Most readers will know some of the references, but few will know all. The question thus arises whether Milton achieves his effect or its opposite. Further, words such as "Adamantine" (48), "durst" (49), "Compeer" (127), "Sovran" (246) and many others, both more and less familiar, add an imposing tone to the work. *Paradise Lost* was not written for an uneducated audience, but in many editions the explanatory notes are almost as long as the text.

Sentence Construction

Besides the references and vocabulary, Milton also tends to use Latinate constructions. English is a syntactical language using word order in sentences to produce sense. Latin, in contrast, is an inflected language in which endings on words indicate the words' functions within a sentence, thereby making word order less important. Latin verbs, for example, often come at the end of the sentence or a direct object may precede the subject. In *Paradise Lost,* Milton seems purposely to strive for atypical English syntactical patterns. He almost never writes in simple sentences. Partly, this type of inverted, at times convoluted, syntax is necessary for the poetics, to maintain the correct meter, but at other times the odd syntax itself seems to be Milton's stylistic goal.

In this passage from Book VIII, the exact meaning of the words is elusive because of the Latinate syntax:

> soft oppression seis'd
> My droused sense, untroubl'd though I thought
> I then was passing to my former state
> Insensible, and forthwith to dissolve (VIII, 291–296).

Lewis, and others who admire the grand style, argue that in passages such as this, the precise meaning matters less than the impressionistic effect, that the images of drowsing, insensibility, and dissolution occurring in order show the breakdown of a conscious mind, in this case Adam's, as God produces a dream vision for him. Certainly this passage, as difficult to understand literally as it is, is not bad writing. The reader understands what Adam is experiencing. However, in the hands of lesser talents than Milton, such writing becomes nonsense.

Extended Similes

Another aspect of Milton's style is the extended simile. The use of epic similes goes back to Homer in the *Iliad* and *Odyssey*, but Milton uses more similes and with more detail. A Miltonic simile can easily become the subject of an essay, perhaps a book. Milton's similes run a gamut from those that seem forced (the comparison of Satan's arrival in Eden to the smell of fish [IV, 166]) to those that are perfect (Eden compared to the field where Proserpine gathered flowers [(IV, 268]). But, in all cases, a critical exploration of the simile reveals depths of unexpected meaning about the objects or persons being compared. Once again, Milton achieves a purpose with his highly involved language and similes. The ability to do this seems almost unique to Milton, a man of immense learning and great poetic ability.

Repeated Images

Besides extended similes, Milton also traces a number of images throughout the poem. One of the most apparent is the image of the maze or labyrinth. Over and over in the poem, there are mentions of mazes—like the tangled curls of Eve's hair—which finally culminate with the serpent confronting Eve on a "Circular base of rising folds, that tow'r'd / Fold above fold a surging maze" (IX, 498–499). Other images also run throughout the poem as a kind of tour de force of imagination and organization. Each image opens up new possibilities for understanding Milton's ideas.

No doubt, particular aspects of Milton's style could be presented at great length, but these are sufficient. Milton intended to write in "a grand style." That style took the form of numerous references and allusions, complex vocabulary, complicated grammatical constructions, and extended similes and images. In consciously doing these things, Milton devised a means of giving the written epic the bardic grandeur of the original recited epic. In so doing, he created an artificial style that very few writers could hope to emulate though many tried. As with the unique styles of William Faulkner and James Joyce, Milton's style is inimitable, and those who try to copy it sometimes give the original a bad name.

Milton's style is certainly his own. Elements of it can be criticized, but in terms of his accomplishment in *Paradise Lost*, it is difficult to see how such a work could be better written in some other style. Milton defined the style of the English epic and, in a real sense, with that style, ended the genre. After Milton and *Paradise Lost*, the English epic ends.

CliffsNotes Review

Use this CliffsNotes Review to test your understanding of the original text and rein-force what you've learned in this book. After you work through the review and essay questions, identify the quote section, and the fun and useful practice projects, you're well on your way to understanding a comprehensive and meaningful interpretation of *Paradise Lost*.

Q&A

1. What purpose does Milton state for *Paradise Lost*?

    a. to show how God defeated the rebellious angels

    b. to justify the ways of God to men

    c. to prove the superiority of Protestantism over Catholicism

2. Who are Satan's daughter and son?

    a. Chaos and Night

    b. Adam and Eve

    c. Sin and Death

3. Who cast the rebellious angels into Hell?

    a. God

    b. the Son

    c. Gabriel

4. From which tree are Adam and Eve prohibited from eating?

    a. Tree of Life

    b. Tree of Knowledge

    c. Tree of Evil

5. After both Adam and Eve have eaten the fruit, what is the first thing they do?

    a. put on clothes

    b. worship the tree

    c. have sex

6. Besides death, what punishment do women receive because of the fall?

    a. to be subservient to men

    b. never to be ordained as ministers

    c. to bear the pain of childbirth

7. Even though God knows what Man will do, he in no way affects Man's choices because Man has _____.

8. _____ is the only one of Satan's followers who does not stay with him in the rebellion.

9. Eve is most surprised by the serpent's ability to _____.

10. God says that the _____ of Eve will eventually bruise the head of the serpent.

11. Michael shows Adam a vision of biblical history from the time of Adam through the birth of _____.

Answers: (1) b. (2) c. (3) b. (4) b. (5) c. (6) c. (7) free will (8) Abdiel (9) talk (10) seed (11) Jesus

Identify the Quote: Find Each Quote in Paradise Lost

1. Of Man's first disobedience, and the fruit
Of that forbidden tree, whose mortal taste
Brought death into the world, and all our woe,
With loss of Eden, till one greater Man
Restore us, and regain the blissful seat,
Sing Heav'nly Muse . . . . (I, 1–3)

2. . . . . what in me is dark
Illumine, what is low raise and support;
That to the hight of this great argument
I may assert Eternal Providence,
And justify the ways of God to men. (I, 22–26)

3. The mind is its own place, and in itself
Can make a heav'n of hell, a hell of heav'n (I, 254–255)

4. Here we may reign secure, and in my choice
To reign is worth ambition though in hell:
Better to reign in hell, than serve in heav'n. (I, 261–263)

5. . . . long is the way
And hard, that out of hell leads up to light; . . . (II, 432-3)

6. . . . which way shall I fly
Infinite wrath, and infinite despair?
Which way I fly is hell; myself am hell;
And in the lowest deep a lower deep,
Still threat'ning to devour me opens wide,
To which the hell I suffer seems a heav'n. (IV, 73–78)

7. Servant of God, well done; well hast thou fought
The better fight . . . . (VI, 29)

8. . . . be lowly wise:
Think only what concerns thee and thy being; . . . . (VIII, 173–174)

9. Earth felt the wound, and nature from her seat,
Sighing through all her works gave signs of woe,
That all was lost. (IX, 782–784)

10. Some natural tears they dropped, but wiped them soon;
The world was all before them, where to choose
Their place of rest, and Providence their guide.
They hand in hand with wand'ring steps and slow,
Through Eden took their solitary way. (XII, 645–650)

Answers: (1) [Milton (the Narrator), calling on the Muse (Urania) to help him write the story of Adam and Eve and their disobedience to God in eating the fruit of the Tree of Knowledge.] (2) [Milton, stating his two great purposes for the poem—to assert eternal Providence and to justify God's ways to men through the story of the fall of Adam and Eve.] (3) [Satan, at his most heroic when he first arrives in Hell, asserting that the mind can control how one deals with circumstances.] (4) [Satan, again on first arriving in Hell, asserting his own free will, unaware of God's power.] (5) [Satan, addressing the council of Demons in Book II, volunteering to leave Hell in order to find God's new creation of Earth and Man.] (6) [Satan, in his soliloquy upon first seeing Earth, describing Hell not only as a place but a state of mind wherein one is alienated from God.] (7) [God, addressing the angel, Abdiel, who stood up to Satan and left the rebellious angels.] (8) [Raphael, to Adam, advising the human not to concern himself with God's ways and motives and to learn the things he most needs to know.] (9) [The Narrator, describing the shock to the universe as Eve eats the forbidden fruit.] (10) [The Narrator, describing Adam's and Eve's departure from Eden and their entry into the world.]

Essay Questions

1. Explain and justify Milton's use of God as a character. Consider how the work would be different if God were not a character.

2. Is it possible to defend the idea that Satan is the true hero of *Paradise Lost*? Explain why or why not.

3. Given the contexts of biography, time, and subject, is Milton an anti-feminist writer? Explain.

4. Who is the hero of *Paradise Lost*? Explain fully.

5. Does Milton's grand style enhance or detract from the power of his story? Be sure to consider ideas from both sides of this argument.

6. What is the purpose of Books XI and XII? Are they necessary for Milton's purpose?

7. How can Milton justify a work which glorifies obedience to authority when he himself supported the overthrow and execution of Charles I?

8. How do Adam and Eve differ before and after the fall?

9. How does Milton use Satan's transformations to reveal character?

10. Compare the "Unholy Trinity" of Satan, Sin, and Death to the "Holy Trinity" of the Son, Adam, and Eve.

Practice Projects

1. Prepare a three-dimensional model or diorama of one of the following: Eden, Hell, Milton's Cosmos.

2. Do a research report on the demons catalogued by Milton in the second part of Book I. Find the historical source for each demon named and any references to that demon in the Bible.

3. Using the Internet, prepare a report using some presentation program, showing and explaining various artistic representations of scenes from *Paradise Lost*.

4. Do a computer presentation comparing Milton's Hell with Dante's. Be sure to include Dante's use of allegory and explain whether allegory enhances or detracts from a depiction of Hell.

CliffsNotes Resource Center

The learning doesn't need to stop here. CliffsNotes Resource Center shows you the best of the best—links to the best information in print and online about the author and / or related works. And don't think that this is all we've prepared for you; we've put all kinds of pertinent information at www.cliffsnotes.com. Look for all the terrific resources at your favorite bookstore or local library and on the Internet. When you're online, make your first stop www.cliffsnotes.com where you'll find more incredibly useful information about *Paradise Lost*.

Books

This CliffsNotes book provides a meaningful interpretation of *Paradise Lost*. If you are looking for information about the author and / or related works, check out these other publications:

Milton: a Biography, by William Riley Parker, is still the best modern biography of Milton. New York: Oxford University Press, 1968.

John Milton. Complete Poems and Major Prose, edited by Merritt Y. Hughes, continues to be the most widely used text of Milton's works. The work has extensive notes and background material and continues to be reprinted in hardback and paperback editions. New York: The Odyssey Press, 1957.

Milton and the Modern Critics, by Robert Martin Adams, is a good, readable account of some of the major critical debates on *Paradise Lost*. This is one of the few books on Milton that uses humor. New York: Cornell University Press, 1955.

Milton: Modern Essays in Criticism, edited by Arthur A. Barker, is good collection of essays on Milton. More than half of the essays are on *Paradise Lost*. New York: Oxford University Press, 1965.

From Virgil to Milton, by C. M. Bowra, is a classic study of the epic form through Milton. London: Macmillan, 1945.

Images of Kingship in Paradise Lost: Milton's Politics and Christian Liberty, by Stevie Davies, discusses *Paradise Lost* in terms of Milton's political thought. Columbia: University of Missouri Press, 1983.

Milton's Theatrical Epic: The Invention and Design of Paradise Lost, by John G. Demaray, considers the dramatic aspects of *Paradise Lost.* Cambridge: Harvard University Press, 1980.

Milton's Imperial Epic: Paradise Lost and the Discourse of Colonialism, by J. Martin Evans, is a recent study of Milton's epic design. New York: Cornell University Press, 1996.

A Preface to Paradise Lost, by C. S. Lewis, is one of the great studies of *Paradise Lost.* Highly readable. London: Oxford University Press, 1942.

Milton: A Collection of Critical Essays, edited by Louis L. Martz, is a solid collection of essays, most of which are on *Paradise Lost.* Englewood Cliffs: Prentice-Hall, 1966.

A Reader's Guide to John Milton, by Marjorie Nicholson, devotes about 140 pages to *Paradise Lost.* Good basic reading of the poem. New York: Farrar, Strauss, Giroux, 1963.

Milton's Grand Style, by Christopher Ricks, is a full study defending Milton's style against critics like T. S. Eliot. New York: Oxford University Press, 1963.

It's easy to find books published by Wiley Publishing, Inc. You'll find them in your favorite bookstores (on the Internet and at a store near you). We also have three Web sites that you can use to read about all the books we publish:

- www.cliffsnotes.com
- www.dummies.com
- www.wiley.com

Internet

Check out these Web resources for more information about John Milton and *Paradise Lost:*

Milton-L Homepage, www.richmond.edu/~creamer/milton/—This site is probably the most complete of all the Milton pages. It contains texts, essays, audio, reviews, and links. It is a basic site for Milton study on the Web. To join the Milton-L discussion group, send an e-mail with the message "subscribe Milton-L" to mailserv@urvax.urich.edu.

The Milton Quarterly, voyager.cns.ohiou.edu/~somalley/milton.html— The Web site of a magazine devoted to Milton studies, it contains critical articles as well as other information and links.

The Milton Review, www.richmond.edu/~creamer/review.html—This site is a source for in-depth reviews of books on Milton and *Paradise Lost*.

The Milton Reading Room, www.dartmouth.edu/~milton/reading_room— This site is the best source for texts of Milton's works. The text of *Paradise Lost* is interactive with good explanations and links on a multitude of words, phrases, and references.

Luminarium—John Milton Page www.luminarium.org/sevenlit/milton— This page is an excellent section of a much larger Web site. Contains links to over 14 essays on *Paradise Lost*. Also contains a biography of Milton and much other information.

Early Modern Literary Studies—Milton's Works and Life: Select Studies and Resources, www.shu.ac.uk/emls/iemls/postprint/CCM2Biblio. html#21—This is essentially an in-depth bibliographic page on everything to do with Milton. Some links to Web sites are included. If you are looking for detailed information on Milton and *Paradise Lost*, this page has the most references.

ELF Presents Milton's Paradise Lost, elf.chaoscafe.com/milton—This site contains a forum on *Paradise Lost* as well as a searchable text.

Paradise Lost Study Guide, www.paradiselost.org—This site includes an online study guide for *Paradise Lost* with links to helpful resources.

John Milton, www.brysons.net/miltonweb/index.html—This is a Web site maintained by a graduate student, which gives cogent reviews and interpretations of many of Milton's philosophical, theological, and political ideas.

The Catholic Encyclopedia, www.newadvent.org/cathen—The Catholic Encyclopedia has scholarly entries on most of the characters mentioned in *Paradise Lost*, as long as they are from the Bible.

Next time you're on the Internet, don't forget to drop by www.cliffsnotes.com. We created an online Resource Center that you can use today, tomorrow, and beyond.

Send Us Your Favorite Tips

In your quest for knowledge, have you ever experienced that sublime moment when you figure out a trick that saves time or trouble? Perhaps you realized you were taking ten steps to accomplish something that could have taken two. Or you found a little-known workaround that achieved great results. If you've discovered a useful resource that gave you insight into or helped you understand *Paradise Lost* and you'd like to share it, the CliffsNotes staff would love to hear from you. Go to our Web site at www.cliffsnotes.com and click the Talk to Us button. If we select your tip, we may publish it as part of CliffsNotes Daily, our exciting, free e-mail newsletter. To find out more or to subscribe to a newsletter, go to www.cliffsnotes.com on the Web.

Index